W9-ANE-003

WITHDRAWN

# EXPLORING AMERICAN HISTORY

## FROM COLONIAL TIMES TO 1877

EDITORS

**Tom Lansford**
*University of Southern Mississippi*

**Thomas E. Woods Jr.**
*Suffolk County Community College, SUNY*

# 3

# Communication – Elections

 **Marshall Cavendish**
Reference
New York

Marshall Cavendish
99 White Plains Road
Tarrytown, New York 10591-9001

www.marshallcavendish.us

© 2008 Marshall Cavendish Corporation

**MARSHALL CAVENDISH**
Editor: Thomas McCarthy
Publisher: Paul Bernabeo
Production Manager: Michael Esposito

**WHITE-THOMSON PUBLISHING**
Editor: Steven Maddocks
Design: Derek Lee and Clare Nicholas
Cartography: Peter Bull Art Studio
Picture Research: Amy Sparks and Clare Collinson
Indexer: Cynthia Crippen, AEIOU, Inc.

**Color key**
- Culture, Society, and Economy
- Government, Politics, War, and Foreign Affairs
- Laws, Treaties, Cases, and Documents
- People
- Places

**Library of Congress Cataloging-in-Publication Data**
Exploring American history : from colonial times to 1877 / editors, Tom Lansford, Thomas E. Woods, Jr.
    p. cm.
    Includes bibliographical references and indexes.
    ISBN 978-0-7614-7746-4 (set : library binding)
    1. United States--History--Colonial period, ca. 1600-1775--Encyclopedias. 2. United States--History--Revolution, 1775-1783--Encyclopedias. 3. United States--History--1783-1865--Encyclopedias. I. Lansford, Tom. II. Woods, Thomas E. III. Title.

E301.E97 2008
973.03--dc22

                                        2007060896

ISBN 978-0-7614-7746-4 (set)
ISBN 978-0-7614-7750-1 (vol. 3)

Printed in China

11 10 09 08 07  5 4 3 2 1

**ILLUSTRATION CREDITS**

**Art Archive:** 278 (Culver Pictures), 288, 311 & 318 (Culver Pictures).

**Bridgeman Art Library:** 228 (Christie's Images), 229 (Peter Newark American Pictures), 237 (Chicago Historical Museum), 250 (American Antiquarian Society, Worcester, MA), 251 (White House, Washington, DC), 255 (Atwater Kent Museum of Philadelphia, Courtesy of Historical Society of Pennsylvania Collection), 260 (Chicago Historical Museum), 261–262 (Peter Newark American Pictures), 272–273 (Chicago Historical Museum), 285 (Archives Charmet), 292 (Schlesinger Library, Radcliffe Institute, Harvard University), 296 (Peter Newark American Pictures), 299 (American Antiquarian Society, Worcester, MA), 300 & 302 (Peter Newark American Pictures), 303 (American Antiquarian Society, Worcester, MA), 308 (Peter Newark American Pictures).

**Corbis:** 230 (PoodlesRock), 243, 244, 253, 256, 258 (Lee Snider/Photo Images), 264 (Randy Faris), 265 (Burstein Collection), 268, 271, 275 (Hulton-Deutsch Collection), 276, 277 (Joseph Sohm; Visions of America), 284 (Krause, Johansen/Archivo Iconografico), 286, 287, 294, 295 (Medford Historical Society Collection), 298, 301 (James P. Blair), 304 (Joseph Sohm; ChromoSohm Inc.), 306, 313 (Stapleton Collection), 316 (Dave G. Houser), 319 (Porter Gifford), 321, 324 (Archivo Iconografico), 326 (David Muench), 329, 330 (Corcoran Gallery of Art).

**Corbis/Bettmann:** 231, 232, 234, 236, 239, 240, 241, 242, 245, 247, 248, 249, 257, 259, 263, 269, 279, 280, 289, 290, 305, 307, 310, 315, 320, 322, 327, 328, 331, 332.

**Library of Congress:** 252, 254, 266, 274, 282, 297, 314, 317.

**Topfoto:** 246 (Joseph Sohm/ImageWorks), 281 (Spectrum/HIP), 325 (ImageWorks).

**COVER:** Abraham Lincoln debates with Stephen A. Douglas in Illinois, lithograph, 1858 (Corbis/Bettmann).

▶ *Delegates to the First Continental Congress (1774) file out of a session in Carpenter's Hall, Philadelphia; 1911 oil painting by Clyde Osmer DeLand* (Bridgeman Art Library/Atwater Kent Museum of Philadelphia/Historical Society of Pennsylvania).

# Contents

| | |
|---|---|
| ● Communication | 228 |
| ● Compromise of 1850 | 234 |
| ● Confederate States of America | 237 |
| ● Constitution of the United States | 246 |
| ● Continental Congresses | 253 |
| ● Cooper, James Fenimore | 260 |
| ● Crockett, David | 263 |
| ● Cuffe, Paul | 266 |
| ● Custer, George Armstrong | 269 |
| ● Davis, Jefferson | 272 |
| ● Declaration of Independence | 277 |
| ● Democracy in America | 284 |
| ● Democratic Party | 287 |
| ● Dix, Dorothea | 292 |
| ● Douglas, Stephen A. | 296 |
| ● Douglass, Frederick | 300 |
| ● Dred Scott v. Sandford | 305 |
| ● Dutch Colonization | 309 |
| ● Education | 315 |
| ● Edwards, Jonathan | 322 |
| ● Elections | 326 |
| ● *Guided Research* | 445 |
| ● *Glossary* | 446 |
| ● *Index* | 447 |

# Communication

IN COLONIAL TIMES settlers did not even have a formal system for the delivery of mail. Few could ever have imagined that one day a letter would travel more than three thousand miles in just two or three days or that instant access to voice communication with people far and wide would be enjoyed by virtually every American.

### Communication by Mail

American colonists in New England had to count on their friends, local merchants, and Native Americans to deliver letters in person, and although the distances from senders to receivers were not great, the process took many days. Similar circumstances existed in the southern colonies, where slaves frequently served as messengers, carrying letters and business papers from one plantation to another. In some cases news about even the most important events, such as the birth of a child or a death in the family, may have taken days or weeks to travel overland.

### Early Post Offices

In 1639 one of the first "post offices" appeared. The General Court of Massachusetts designated a Boston tavern owned by one Richard Fairbanks as the initial location for handling the post. In the

▶ *The Wayside Inn, which stood beside the Boston Post Road in Sudbury, Massachusetts, opened in 1716. It was popularized in Longfellow's* Tales of a Wayside Inn *and is depicted in this oil on canvas,* Wayside Inn on Route to Philadelphia, *by Thomas Birch (1779–1851).*

years that followed, taverns, coffeehouses, and general stores would all become popular locations for messengers to leave and collect correspondence. It was not very long before colonists were able to send mail to friends and family in places as far away as England, the Netherlands, and Sweden (places from which the colonists had come) and receive mail in return.

By 1673 messengers were traveling the Old Boston Post Road, which linked Boston with New York. Ten years later, in 1683, Pennsylvania added a post office, and by 1692 the first centralized postal system in the colonies began to be formed, with the New Jersey governor, Andrew Hamilton, serving as deputy postmaster for the Englishman Thomas Neale, who had received from the British crown a twenty-one-year grant to establish a central postal system along the eastern seaboard of North America. To that end, on May 1, 1693, the Internal Colonial Postal Union began a weekly service that linked Portsmouth, New Hampshire, and Williamsburg, Virginia. The union failed to turn a profit, though; there was not sufficient postal business along the hundreds of coastal miles.

In 1707 the British government bought the postal system that had been serving

North America and took formal charge of it; the crown periodically appointed a colonial deputy postmaster general to run it. Among those who filled that post were John Hamilton, Andrew Hamilton's son; John Lloyd, of Charleston, South Carolina; and Alexander Spotswood, of Virginia.

▲ *This 1795 engraving, from Isaac Weld's* Travels through the States of North America, *depicts an eighteenth-century stagecoach. A fleet of such coaches once delivered American mail.*

## ANDREW HAMILTON ■ DIED 1703

Born in Scotland, Andrew Hamilton worked as a young man in Edinburgh before coming to America as a special agent for the proprietors of the colony of East Jersey (the northeastern part of what became New Jersey). In March 1692 Hamilton was appointed the governor of both West and East Jersey. Also in that year he began to organize a postal service, the first in the American colonies.

In 1697, because of the vagaries of English politics, Parliament removed Hamilton from the governorship, but his successor, Jeremiah Basse, proved so inept that Hamilton was reappointed in August 1699. He served as governor till 1703, when he died. (This Andrew Hamilton is not the same man as the lawyer who represented John Peter Zenger in the 1734 trial in New York that was a milestone in the history of the free press. That man was an unrelated younger contemporary of the governor.)

*This postcard commemorates the events of the night of April 18, 1775, when Paul Revere, a silversmith and champion of the Revolutionary cause, made a famous ride from Charlestown, Massachusetts, inland to Lexington to warn his fellow colonists of apparently aggressive maneuvers by the British redcoats. Forewarned, the American militias were able to repel the British troops the following day.*

Spotswood, who served as deputy postmaster general from 1730 to 1739, appointed the thirty-one-year-old Benjamin Franklin as deputy postmaster of Philadelphia in 1737. Franklin became one of the most important individuals to work in the postal system; he organized routes and increased the efficiency of the service. In addition, his experiments with electricity, especially his development of the lightning rod in 1752, were to have enormous significance in the history of communication. Franklin held the Philadelphia post until 1753 and then served as deputy postmaster general in that year and the next.

## Delivering the Mail by Stagecoach and Pony

In the summer of 1775, a year before independence was declared, the Second Continental Congress, meeting in Philadelphia, agreed to establish a new colonial post office department. The con-gress appointed Benjamin Franklin the first postmaster general of the new department. Later, in 1785, while the independent American states were associated with one another under the Articles of Confederation, Congress authorized the postmaster general, Ebenezer Hazard, to negotiate with stagecoach companies to carry the mail along designated routes. With the success of the stagecoach postal delivery system, post offices sprang up rapidly, their number increasing from 75 in 1790 to 28,498 by 1860. In 1860 riders for the Pony Express began delivering mail along a route that ran 1,966 miles from Saint Joseph, Missouri, to Sacramento, California. Such a remarkable increase was no more than a necessary step to keep pace with the country's growth: during the same period the U.S. population grew from 3.9 million to 31.4 million, and large numbers of people had begun to move west, whether in search of gold, land, or simply a new life. Indeed, when Horace Greeley, the publisher of the *New York Tribune,* famously wrote, "Go west, young man," many ambitious young Americans followed his advice.

Like the Internal Colonial Postal Union of earlier times, however, the Pony Express did not succeed financially, and it went out of business in 1866. The emergence of the telegraph as a form of communication contributed to the economic downturn of the Pony Express. In 1861 the Western Union Company built its first transcontinental telegraph. In 1862 President Abraham Lincoln signed the Pacific Railroad Act, which assigned the Union Pacific and the Central Pacific to build a transcontinental railroad. The railroad, which carried mail and passengers farther and faster than any

PAUL REVERE'S RIDE, APRIL 18, 1775.

horse, would ultimately stretch some 1,700 miles, from Omaha, Nebraska, to Sacramento, California.

## The Telegraph

In the 1830s the inventor Samuel Morse demonstrated that electricity could be used to transmit messages and began experimenting with ways to communicate by means of magnetic wire. By the 1840s the telegraph, along with its indispensable "language," the Morse code, had emerged as a significant form of communication. In 1843 the U.S. Congress allocated $30,000 toward the construction of an experimental forty-mile telegraph wire from Washington, DC, to Baltimore, Maryland. As the historians David Crowley and Paul Heyer described the situation, the telegraph moved communication from a "transportation" model to a "transmission" one. Clerks trained in Morse code sent messages across the lands using a system of dots and dashes. The much greater speeds at which telegraphed news traveled proved too much for messengers on horseback, such as riders for the Pony Express, to compete with.

*On May 24, 1844, Samuel Morse dispatched the first telegraphic message over the experimental line strung from Washington to Baltimore. Drawn from the Old Testament book of Numbers (23:23), the message was suggested to Morse by the young daughter of a friend, a girl named Annie Ellworth.*

*What hath God wrought?*

▼ *Samuel F. B. Morse (1791–1872), who invented the first practical telegraph, is depicted in this unattributed illustration sending the first public telegram in May 1844. The message was sent from the Supreme Court chamber in the Capitol at Washington over a forty-mile wire to Baltimore, Maryland.*

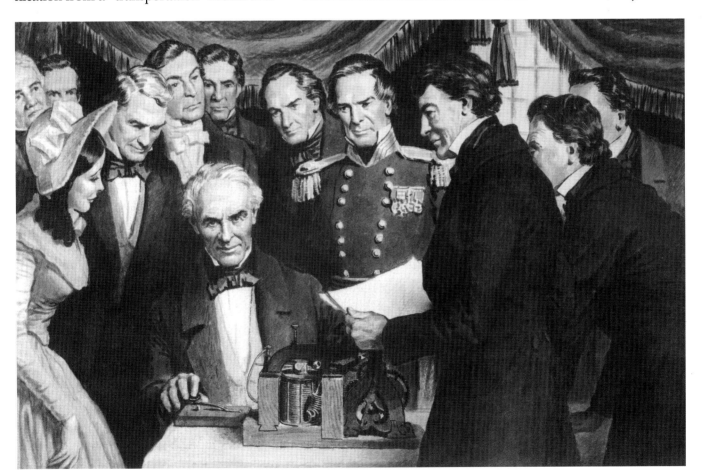

## The Telephone

As significant as the telegraph would become, however, it too met its match when an even better form of communication, the telephone, came along in the 1870s. In March 1876 Alexander Graham Bell constructed his first telephone. Bell had been supported in his research and experiments by his father-in-law, Gardiner Hubbard, as well as Thomas Sanders, the father of one of Bell's students. The three men formed the Bell Telephone Company in 1877, and within a year the first telephone switchboard had appeared in New Haven, Connecticut. The biggest telegraphic company, Western Union, also began offering a telephone service, and Bell filed suit against Western Union for a patent violation. Unsurprising to relate, litigation lasted for a considerable time. It did not, though, alter the primary fact: a new form of electronic communication had been established, and as the twentieth

▲ *Alexander Graham Bell's invention of the telephone in the 1870s revolutionized American communication, which had until then been restricted by the technological limitations of the telegraph. In this photograph Bell demonstrates his invention.*

## CHRONOLOGY

**1639**
A Boston tavern becomes the first post office.

**1673**
Messengers travel the Old Boston Post Road between Boston and New York.

**1683**
Pennsylvania establishes a post office.

**1693**
The Internal Colonial Postal Union is formed and begins weekly service in the colonies.

**1707**
The postal system is bought by the British government.

**1730**
The British government appoints Alexander Spotswood the deputy postmaster general.

**1737**
Spotswood appoints Benjamin Franklin the deputy postmaster of Philadelphia.

**1752**
Franklin proves that lightning is an electrical phenomenon.

**1775**
The Continental Congress appoints Benjamin Franklin the first postmaster general of the new Post Office Department.

**1827**
Baltimore merchants charter the first railroad in North America, the Baltimore & Ohio.

**1830s**
Inventors discover that electricity can be used to transmit messages.

**1840s**
Clerks begin using Morse code to transmit messages by telegraph.

**1860–1861**
Pony Express riders carry the mail along a 1,966-mile route, from St. Joseph, Missouri, to Sacramento, California.

**1861**
The Western Union Company builds the first transcontinental telegraph.

**1862**
Abraham Lincoln signs the Pacific Railroad Act, whereby the Union Pacific and the Central Pacific companies are assigned to build a 1,700-mile transcontinental railroad.

**1876**
Alexander Graham Bell constructs his first telephone.

**1877**
The Bell Telephone Company is created.

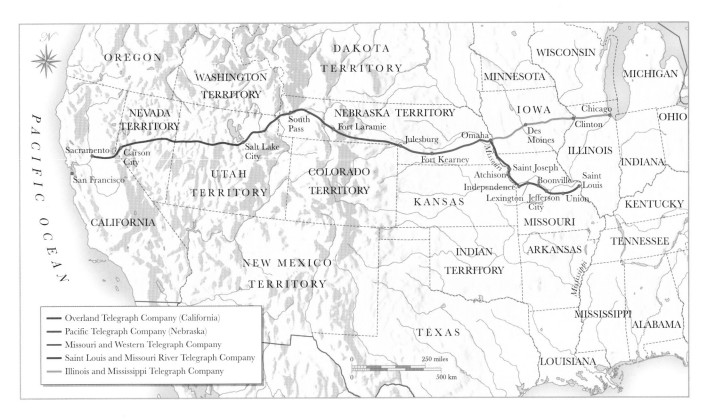

OREGON

WASHINGTON
TERRITORY

NEVADA
TERRITORY

Sacramento
Carson
City

San Francisco

CALIFORNIA

PACIFIC OCEAN

South
Pass

Salt Lake
City

UTAH
TERRITORY

DAKOTA
TERRITORY

NEBRASKA TERRITORY

Fort Laramie

Julesburg

Omaha

Fort Kearney

COLORADO
TERRITORY

KANSAS

WISCONSIN

MINNESOTA

IOWA

Des
Moines

Missouri

Atchison
Independence
Lexington

Chicago
Clinton

ILLINOIS

Saint Joseph
Boonville

Jefferson
City

Union

Saint
Louis

MICHIGAN

OHIO

INDIANA

KENTUCKY

MISSOURI

TENNESSEE

NEW MEXICO
TERRITORY

INDIAN
TERRITORY

ARKANSAS

Mississippi

MISSISSIPPI

ALABAMA

TEXAS

250 miles

500 km

LOUISIANA

— Overland Telegraph Company (California)
— Pacific Telegraph Company (Nebraska)
— Missouri and Western Telegraph Company
— Saint Louis and Missouri River Telegraph Company
— Illinois and Mississippi Telegraph Company

**On March 10, 1876, in Boston, Alexander Graham, Bell, having heard encouraging sounds through the wires he and his assistant, Thomas A. Watson, had strung, excitedly called out the first words ever transmitted telephonically. (The popular story that Bell had spilled acid on himself and was calling for help is unfounded.)**

*Watson, come here. I want you.*

century grew near, people were speaking directly to one another across long distances by telephone.

## Meeting and Creating Needs

From earliest times, people have sought and found ways to transmit information to others—whether by means of messenger-based mail systems, the transportation of parcels by railroads, or the transmission of

messages by such electronic means as the telegraph and telephone. With each advance in speed and convenience has come a concomitant growth in the volume of communication and in the perceived need for further improvement. Although the communication systems of yesteryear did not allow people to take or transmit pictures or check stock prices on cellular telephones and advanced handheld devices, the systems that were in place were, to the degree that they were successful in transmitting news and information, just as integral and vital to daily life.

*Bryan E. Denham*

**SEE ALSO**

• Franklin, Benjamin • Greeley, Horace
• Hamilton, Alexander
• Morse, Samuel F. B. • Pony Express
• Press • Revere, Paul
• Union Pacific Railroad

▲ *The western portion of the route of the first transcontinental telegraph line, completed by the Western Union Company in October 1861. The line built by the Saint Louis and Missouri River Telegraph Company in 1851 provided the original link with the East. However, following the outbreak of the Civil War, this line was subject to disruption, and so the Illinois and Mississippi Telegraph Company built a new branch line to the north.*

# Compromise of 1850

THE COMPROMISE OF 1850 consisted of a series of legislative measures adopted by Congress in September of that year. Its intent was to address several slavery-related issues that were worsening relations between the states of the North and the South.

▼ *An unattributed oil of Henry Clay, who played a decisive role in bringing about the Missouri Compromise of 1820 but campaigned unsuccessfully for the passage of the various provisions of the Compromise of 1850 in a single omnibus bill.*

Slavery had been a divisive issue from the very beginnings of the American republic. A balance among free and slave states, which was vital to the interests of the southern states, had been maintained during westward expansion. By virtue of the proportional representation in the House of Representatives, the South, a mostly rural region, had little chance of acquiring a majority in that chamber. In the Senate, however, each state's representation was the same. So long as the number of free and slave states remained equal, southern senators felt secure in their ability to protect their region's interests.

## Striving for Balance

In 1820 Henry Clay spearheaded the Missouri Compromise, which allowed the territory to enter the Union as a slave state. The measure also approved the creation of the free state of Maine (till then part of Massachusetts), and so the balance in the Senate was maintained and confrontation avoided. By 1850, however, new issues had arisen, and again, North and South were on opposite sides.

The first bone of contention was California statehood. Thanks to its rapid growth, partly as a result of the gold rush, in 1849 California requested admission into the Union as a free state. With the balance in the Senate of free and slave states threatened, most southern states were opposed to the request. However, southerners' long-standing concern about the lack of enforcement of the 1793 Fugitive Slave Law led to a compromise. In exchange for their support of California's admission as a free state, a stronger fugitive slave law was added to the provisions of the Compromise of 1850.

*The reaction of the abolitionist Frederick Douglass to the Compromise of 1850 and to all who supported it was widely shared.*

*The ruling parties of the country have now flung off all disguises, and have openly and shamelessly declared war upon the only saving principles known to nations. [They] embrace the whole slave system, as worthy of their regard and support.*

AN ADDRESS GIVEN IN ITHACA, NEW YORK,
OCTOBER 14, 1852

## Aftermath of the Mexican War

The United States acquired a vast amount of territory in 1848 following victory in the Mexican War, and it was uncertain whether that territory would be free or slave. Furthermore, Texas laid claim to land as far west as Santa Fe. Under the Compromise of 1850, Texas was awarded ten million dollars to renounce its claim to the western land. The territories of Utah and New Mexico were organized out of this land, and the issue of slavery in these territories was left to be determined by popular sovereignty; that is, the citizens—strictly speaking, the territorial legislators—would decide for or against permitting slavery when they applied for statehood.

## Slave Trading in Washington, DC

Slavery was legal in the District of Columbia; indeed, the district had become one of the largest slave-trade venues on the continent. This state of affairs concerned some southern congressmen, who feared that foreign leaders, witnessing slave auctions in the capital, might carry reports of these distressing sights back to their homeland and add fuel to abolitionist pressures. The compromise abolished the slave trade in the district without prohibiting slavery.

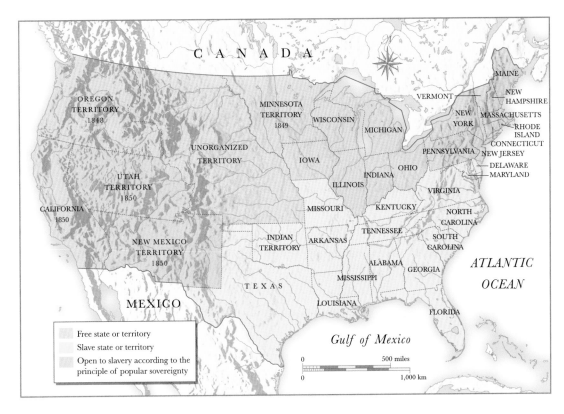

◀ *The Compromise of 1850 achieved a shaky balance between the interests of America's pro- and anti-slavery factions. Within four years, however, the Kansas-Nebraska Act, by allowing for slavery (according to popular sovereignty) in a region where it had previously been prohibited by the Missouri Compromise, propelled the nation toward war.*

235

*Stephen Douglas, the subject of this undated engraving, navigated the provisions of the Compromise of 1850 through Congress by introducing them one at a time so that shifting majorities could support only the planks they favored.*

## Doomed from the Outset

Two things were clear in Washington in 1850: virtually no one wanted to compromise on his principles, and virtually everyone sought to forestall deepening sectional bitterness or, worse, secession. It is hardly any wonder, therefore, that the agreed-upon compromise—largely the

**In the course of Senate debate with Daniel Webster of Massachusetts, Stephen Douglas stated his goals and desires for the compromise and for the nation:**

*We know the responsibilities that devolve upon us. . . . We indulge in no ultraisms—no sectional strifes—no crusades against the North or the South. Our aim will be to do justice to all, to all men, to every section. We are prepared to fulfill all our obligations under the Constitution as it is, and determined to maintain and preserve it inviolate in its letter and spirit.*

result of the tireless efforts of Senator Stephen A. Douglas of Illinois to reach some sort of agreement, no matter how tenuous or fragile—was respected by few and loved by none. Even popular sovereignty, which the more populist-minded legislators found very appealing, soon lost its luster. In 1854, when the Kansas and Nebraska territories were formed, the application to them of popular sovereignty effectively abrogated the last vestiges of the Missouri Compromise. The well-nigh predictable result was Bleeding Kansas.

*Brian A. Carriere*

**SEE ALSO**
- Abolitionism • Brown, John
- Clay, Henry • Douglas, Stephen A.
- Fugitive Slave Laws • Gold Rushes
- Kansas-Nebraska Act • Mexican War
- Missouri Compromise
- Popular Sovereignty • Slavery
- States' Rights • Texas
- Underground Railroad
- Webster, Daniel • Wilmot Proviso

# Confederate States of America

SOUTHERN STATES began to withdraw from the Union in 1860, and as they did, they began to forge a political identity, which became the Confederate States of America (the CSA), or the Confederacy.

## Origins of the Confederacy

Southern leaders appealed to the spirit of the Declaration of Independence to justify their withdrawal from the Union. As they saw it, the North, not the South, had departed from the principles that had inspired the American Revolution. For decades southern political theorists, notably John C. Calhoun, had argued that the Revolution's primary objective was to create not a large unitary country with an all-powerful central government but instead a group of self-governing and independent states that associated freely and fraternally with one another.

Many southerners adopted the "compact" view of constitutionalism. According to this view, traceable to resolutions passed in Kentucky and Virginia in 1798, the Constitution was a compact between the principals—that is, the states—and their agent, the federal government. The sovereign states had delegated powers to a national government and could withdraw from this compact, or union, if they deemed it necessary to do so.

In any event, by 1860 the shaky balance of power between southern state governments and the national government had beeen upset. A critical event leading to secession was the rise of the new Republican Party, among whose founding principles was total opposition to slavery. With the election in 1860 of the Republican presidential candidate, Abraham Lincoln,

coupled with the emergence of a clear majority of free states admitted to the Union and represented in Congress, many came to agree with the murderous abolitionist John Brown, who prophesied, just before his hanging in 1859, that blood must be spilled before the issue of slavery would be resolved.

▼ *Although he died in 1850, John C. Calhoun (pictured here in 1845 in a portrait by James Reid Lambdin) was one architect of the Confederacy. He argued that each sovereign state had the right to govern itself in everything but those few areas over which it had delegated its powers to the federal government.*

## Secession

South Carolina was the first state to secede from the Union, on December 20, 1860. By February 1861 six more states had followed: Mississippi, Florida, Alabama, Georgia, Louisiana, and Texas. By summer North Carolina, Virginia, Arkansas, and Tennessee had seceded. Missouri and Kentucky also formed secessionist governments in the fall of 1861, but those states' official governments remained loyal to the Union. In addition to these states, the five tribal governments in the Indian Territory (later Oklahoma) offered their support to the Confederacy as well. The southern portion of Arizona Territory also successfully petitioned the Confederate government for annexation. Two other slave states, Maryland and Delaware, were persuaded (or compelled) not to secede.

## The Formation of the Confederacy

The seceding states understood that they had to demonstrate political viability in order to sustain their independence. Not only did they have to repel a northern invasion, but they also had to show friends and foes alike that they were competent to govern themselves. Doing so required the formation of central governmental structures and associated institutions, development of diplomatic relationships with foreign nations, and the maintenance of social order and economic stability. The CSA's official formation took place on February 4, 1861. According to the 1860 U.S. census, the new Confederacy numbered some 9 million people, of whom 3.5 million were slaves.

On March 11 the Confederate constitution was ratified. It adopted language drawn from the Articles of Confederation and (especially with respect to government structure) the document it superseded, the U.S. Constitution. Its distinctive features included strong protection of the rights of states to govern themselves, protection of the institution of slavery (though it

*▼ The Confederate States of America officially came into existence on February 4, 1861. On July 15, 1870, when Georgia became the last former Confederate state to be readmitted to the Union, the Confederacy officially ceased to exist.*

**The preamble to the Confederate constitution resembles and differs from the U.S. Constitution's preamble in interesting ways.**

*We, the people of the Confederate States, each State acting in its sovereign and independent character, in order to form a permanent federal government, establish justice, insure domestic tranquillity, and secure the blessings of liberty to ourselves and our posterity—invoking the favor and guidance of Almighty God—do ordain and establish this Constitution for the Confederate States of America.*

outlawed slave importation), a ban on protective tariffs (a major grievance of the southern states), and specific reference to "Almighty God" as the nation's ultimate source of legitimacy. The Confederate president was elected for a single six-year term and, unlike the U.S. president, had a line-item veto (the power to veto specific items in a bill while signing the rest into law). The Confederate constitution did not mention the right of a state to secede; southerners believed this was an inherent right needing no formal recognition. The Confederacy's first capital was Montgomery, Alabama, but Richmond, Virginia, became the capital in May 1861. Jefferson Davis, a native Kentuckian who had served as secretary of war and a U.S. senator from Mississippi, was elected its president.

## Economic History

The economy of the antebellum South was almost totally agrarian. Indeed, prior to the Civil War only 10 percent of the nation's manufactured goods were produced in the South. For this reason, the economy of the Confederacy was on unsure footing when the conflict began. Manufacturing had essentially to be invented to produce war materials. Furthermore, cotton production, the South's primary means of sustenance, fell from 4.5 million bales in 1860 to 300,000 in 1864. The disruptions of war,

▲ *This anonymous illustration shows people gathering in Montgomery, Alabama, for the inauguration of Jefferson Davis as president of the Confederacy.*

especially the Union naval blockade, cut the Confederate economy off from much-needed foreign trade.

At first, Confederate leaders believed that other countries were so dependent upon southern cotton that they would be forced to assist the Confederacy in its struggle for independence. Early in the war some southerners even deliberately disengaged from trade with Europe to hasten foreign intervention. However, European governments found other ways of dealing with the shortage, and eventually, just to survive, the South was forced to sell its cotton to Europe any way it could (often by blockade-running).

As the economy sagged, Confederate war financing suffered. Financing was also limited in other ways. Prior to the war, taxes were lowest in the American South. Southerners had no history of paying high taxes and would not welcome a tax increase, and the Confederate government had severely limited taxing powers. The Confederate constitution, like the Articles of Confederation, made tax assessment and collection duties primarily of state governments. Relying upon state governments to supply revenue proved frustrating for Davis and the Confederate Congress.

Alternative methods of financing the war were hardly better. Though the Confederate treasury sold war bonds throughout the war, the high inflation rate made the bonds increasingly unattractive. The government ended up paying for the war by printing more and more dollars, which rapidly lost value, and by borrowing.

The weak economy had its most immediate impact in the home. With the young men off fighting, the women and children had to put food on the table. Planting, harvesting, and selling had to continue if southern families were to eat. Meanwhile, the blockade made basic household necessities, including food, ever scarcer. Scarcity in turn contributed to inflation, which led to civil unrest, including a "bread revolt" in Richmond in the middle of the war.

*An unattributed head-and-shoulders portrait of Jefferson Davis, the first and only president of the Confederate States of America. Although Davis had opposed secession in the years leading up to the war, he consistently defended the states' right to secede from the Union.*

## CHRONOLOGY

**1860**
Abraham Lincoln is elected president; South Carolina secedes in December.

**January 1861**
Mississippi secedes, followed by Florida, Alabama, Georgia, and Louisiana.

**February 1861**
Texas secedes.

**March 1861**
The Confederate constitution is ratified; Jefferson Davis and Alexander Stephens are elected president and vice president, respectively.

**April 1861**
Virginia secedes; war begins as shots are fired at Fort Sumter, South Carolina.

**May–June 1861**
Arkansas, North Carolina, and Tennessee secede.

**July 1863**
The Confederacy suffers turning-point defeats at Vicksburg and Gettysburg.

**November 1864**
Lincoln is reelected.

**April 1865**
Richmond falls; Lee surrenders to Grant at Appomattox Court House, Virginia.

**By 1870**
All former Confederate states have been readmitted to the Union.

## Government

Most accounts hold that the Confederate government was made up of undistinguished men—a surprising assessment, given the remarkable legacy of George Washington, Patrick Henry, Thomas Jefferson, Andrew Jackson, John C. Calhoun, and Henry Clay. Most of the South's human talent, however, went into the military, not politics. Nowhere was this situation more evident than in the Confederate Congress. Its members, compared with their Union counterparts, lacked legislative experience. Even worse, Confederate congressmen gained a reputation for poor character. Numerous floor fights and instances of public drunkenness contributed to Confederate voters' declining confidence in the body, which most historians have judged reactionary and ineffective. Nor has the Confederate cabinet garnered high marks for its performance either then or since. With frequent shifts and resignations, sixteen different men served in the cabinet's six positions over the four years of war.

◀ *The Confederate battle flag was flown from late 1861 through the end of the war. Its thirteen stars represent the states of the Confederacy—the eleven states that joined formally plus Missouri and Kentucky. In these two states, which had representatives in both the U.S. and the Confederate congresses, much Confederate sympathy existed; both supplied regiments to the Southern cause.*

### THE CONFEDERATE FLAG

The official CSA flag is called the Stars and Bars (a description of its appearance). Since the flag's similarity to the Union flag, the Stars and Stripes, made it unfit for battlefield use, Confederates adopted a flag whose design was based on the Southern Cross for military operations; it is still the more familiar of the two Confederate flags. Both used stars to represent the member states.

▲ *This contemporary engraving depicts Confederate President Jefferson Davis, surrounded by members of his cabinet, signing government papers by the roadside.*

President Jefferson Davis, too, has suffered at historians' hands, especially compared with Abraham Lincoln. Davis has been called a proud and ill-tempered man who was unwilling to compromise on even minor points. Throughout the war Davis suffered constant and open criticism from the southern press and from key politicians, including Joseph Brown, the governor of Georgia, and even members of his own cabinet. Among his most outspoken critics was his own vice president, Alexander Stephens. One must acknowledge, however, that Davis was faced with the daunting task of leading a nation born in crisis, a nation defined and often frustrated by its institutional disunity—that is, it was a true confederacy, not a consolidated state.

**Foreign Affairs**

Before the war southern leaders believed they had European friends in high places. The South, as they saw it, needed only to show some viability in self-governance and demonstrate that it could compete militarily. Dependence upon southern cotton would persuade European countries to intervene, or so the Confederacy thought. At the very least, the Confederate government expected to gain diplomatic recognition from France and Britain.

The Union, never recognizing the legitimacy of the Confederate government, refused to declare war on the Confederacy. The Confederate Congress, on the other hand, officially declared war on the Union as an expression of its self-perception as a sovereign state. Although several foreign countries received many CSA diplomats, Confederate diplomatic efforts ultimately achieved very little. France did appoint a consul to the Confederate government in 1861, but this act did not amount to diplomatic recognition. After early Confederate battlefield successes, Britain took some steps toward formal recognition, but both Britain and France backed off when the Confederacy suffered setbacks at Antietam, Gettysburg, and Vicksburg.

▼ *The home of Alexander H. Stephens, vice president of the Confederacy, was undamaged during the Civil War. Located in Crawfordville, Georgia, it is a historic site that to this day attracts a great many visitors.*

## ALEXANDER STEPHENS ■ 1812–1883

Alexander Stephens, born into a poor Georgia family, was fortunate enough to have his education and law degree financed by a benefactor. Though Stephens opposed secession, he had been an ardent advocate of states' rights while serving Georgia as a U.S. congressman. Having helped draft the new Confederate constitution, he was elected vice president.

Stevens's unswerving support of states' rights often put him at odds with the Confederate Congress and President Davis. To Stephens these rights were sacred, never to be compromised, not even during times of crisis. When Davis resorted to conscription (a draft), Stephens spoke out against loyalty to that government: "A citizen of the state has no allegiance to the Confederate States government . . . and can owe no military service to it except as required by his own state."

After the war Stephens served six months in prison before being released. His home state promptly elected him to the U.S. House of Representatives, but the Republican-controlled Congress refused to seat him or other former Confederates. He finally won the right to take his seat in the early 1870s and left only to serve as governor of Georgia. Stephens spent the rest of his life defending the South's actions on constitutional grounds.

## JUDAH P. BENJAMIN  ■  1811–1884

Judah Benjamin is widely considered the most competent member of the Confederate government. Born to Jewish parents, Benjamin grew up in the Carolinas and settled in New Orleans as a young man. He made his fortune as a sugar planter and lawyer and was elected to the U.S. Senate, where he served from 1852 until Louisiana seceded in 1861. Quickly appointed to the Davis cabinet, he served first as attorney general, then as secretary of war and secretary of state. Benjamin, known for his strong commitment to Confederate independence, urged Davis to emancipate all southern slaves in order to win the affection of an antislavery Europe. Benjamin became one of Davis's closest friends and most trusted subordinates. Indeed, Benjamin stayed with Davis until the latter's capture and then escaped to England, where he made a name for himself as a lawyer. He died there in 1884.

By the end of 1863, it was clear, despite the efforts of the CSA secretary of state, Judah Benjamin, that European countries would take a position of neutrality only.

**The Final Days of the Confederacy**

On Sunday, April 2, 1865, Jefferson Davis received word that General Robert E. Lee's army was heavily outnumbered and surrounded and losing members hourly; Richmond could fall to Union troops at any moment. These fears were confirmed when a courier brought Davis a dispatch from Lee: "I think it is absolutely necessary that we should abandon our position to-night. . . ." Davis reluctantly set out to transport the capital elsewhere. By the next afternoon the Confederate government had been loaded onto several train cars and was steaming away from a city in flames, with anything that could be of use to the enemy (including thousands of pages of government documents) fueling the fire.

Late efforts to secure peace between the North and the South had failed in February—three Confederate commissioners, including the vice president, met with Lincoln without achieving an acceptable compromise—but Davis was still convinced, however unrealistically, that victory was

▲ *An unattributed photograph of Judah Benjamin, who fled to England after the Civil War and enjoyed a successful and lucrative second career as a barrister. His* Treatise on the Law of Sale of Personal Property *(1868) is considered a classic of its field.*

still possible and that the fall of Richmond and even the surrender of Lee's forces in Virginia were only temporary setbacks. The government would simply relocate, and troops would be reorganized to fight on elsewhere. With Sherman forcing the surrender of Confederate forces in the Southeast, however, Confederate hopes evaporated in the spring of 1865. Davis himself was captured in Irwinville, Georgia, on May 9. He was imprisoned under often cruel and degrading conditions for two years.

**An Enduring Legacy**

The Confederacy outlived its short life in several ways. Though no state has attempted to secede from the Union since 1861, the constitutional arguments in favor of states' rights continue to feature in debates involving the American system of federalism. One particularly volatile example concerns resistance to legally mandated racial equality, which endured at least a century after the Civil War; in the 1950s politicians and others could be heard using many of the same arguments Confederate leaders had used.

The Confederacy lives on in the hearts and minds of many southerners to this day. The lives of such leaders as Stonewall Jackson, Robert E. Lee, and Jefferson Davis continue to be celebrated—and not just in the South. Debates over whether and to what extent the story of the Confederacy should be honored or remembered as a sore spot in American history also persist, especially with respect to Confederate monuments and the state flags that explicitly refer to the Confederacy.

*Troy Gibson*

▲ *This 1866 lithograph by Thomas Kelly depicts Jefferson Davis and his cabinet in the Council Chamber at Richmond with General Robert E. Lee. Pictured from left to right are Secretary of the Navy Stephen R. Mallory, Attorney General Judah P. Benjamin, Secretary of War Leroy Pope Walker, President Jefferson Davis, General Robert E. Lee, Postmaster General John H. Reagan, Secretary of the Treasury Christopher G. Memminger, Vice President Alexander H. Stephens, and Secretary of State Robert Toombs.*

SEE ALSO
• Articles of Confederation
• Calhoun, John C. • Clay, Henry
• Davis, Jefferson
• Emancipation Proclamation
• Jackson, Thomas J. • Lee, Robert E.
• Revolutionary War

# Constitution of the United States

SINCE 1789 THE CONSTITUTION has served as the governing document for the United States of America. In ratifying this document, the states created a national, or "general," government with defined powers and allowed the placement of limits on state power.

## Articles of Confederation

The thirteen original American states were united and governed under the Articles of Confederation from 1781 until the implementation of the Constitution in 1789. Although the Confederation government presided over the successful prosecution of the American Revolution and the acquisition of vast new territory from the western side of the Appalachian Mountains to the Mississippi River, many Americans believed that a more energetic general government was needed.

The Confederation government lacked certain critical powers. For example, if the Confederation needed money, Congress could not tax the people; it could only ask the state legislatures for funding. Without a predictable stream of revenue, the Confederation had trouble paying its debts and might have been unable to obtain loans in an emergency.

In the realm of foreign affairs, other countries were reluctant to deal with the Confederation Congress because it could not ensure that the individual states and their citizens would respect treaty obligations. Congress also lacked the power to persuade foreign nations to comply with existing duties or to respect American rights.

## Calling a Convention

In March 1785 delegates from Maryland and Virginia met at George Washington's

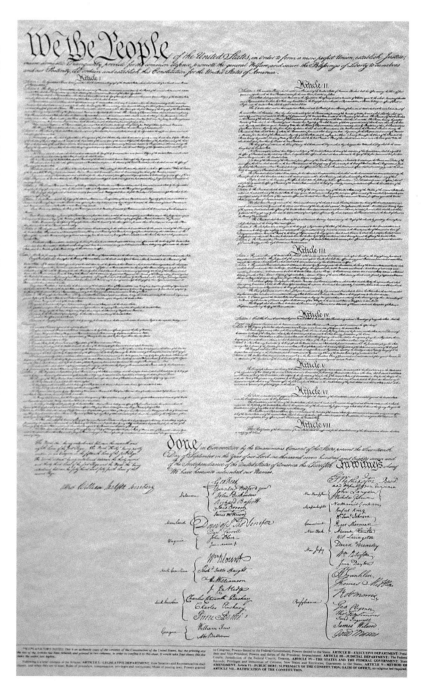

The original United States Constitution, on its faded parchment paper. This document, drafted in 1787, is the oldest written constitution still in effect anywhere in the world.

home at Mount Vernon, Virginia, to settle a dispute over the navigation of the Potomac River. This conference raised broader questions about the regulation of trade between the American states. The Virginia legislature then invited all thirteen states to send delegates to Annapolis, Maryland, to consider a wide range of commercial matters.

The Annapolis Convention met in September 1786, but only five states sent delegates. Believing strongly that reform was badly needed, the delegates suggested that another convention be held the next year in Philadelphia. James Madison, a Virginia delegate present in Annapolis, drafted Virginia's invitation to the other states to assemble and consider "the Exigencies of the Union." Following Virginia's lead, the Confederation Congress endorsed the idea of a convention meeting for the "purpose of revising the Articles of Confederation."

▲ *An anonymous engraving of the state house in Philadelphia, where the Constitutional Convention was held in the summer of 1787.*

## ARTICLE I

Article I of the Constitution vests the legislative power in the Congress of the United States, a bicameral body consisting of the House of Representatives and the Senate. Under the terms of what is known as the Great Compromise, in the House representation is based on population, whereas in the Senate it is the same for all the states.

The Philadelphia convention rejected a proposal to grant Congress a general power of legislation and instead drafted a list of powers. The Constitution's enumeration of congressional powers contains many that also appeared in the Articles of Confederation: borrowing money, fixing standards of weights and measures, establishing post offices and post roads, regulating trade with the Indian tribes, and declaring war. Additional powers include authority to lay and collect taxes, duties, imposts, and excises; to pass naturalization and bankruptcy laws; and to regulate commerce with foreign nations and between the states. Following the enumeration is the so-called Necessary and Proper Clause, which permits Congress to pass all laws necessary and proper for the execution of the enumerated powers.

The power to regulate commerce was much debated at the convention. The southern states, which primarily exported goods, feared oppressive taxation on exports and a prohibition of the slave trade. Hence, they demanded a two-thirds vote in Congress before a commercial regulation could became law. A compromise was reached that prohibited Congress from interfering with the slave trade until 1808 and from ever taxing exports. With these protections in place and the South's principal immediate concerns having been met, southern opposition to a commerce power based on a majority vote disappeared.

## Making a Beginning

Delegates began arriving in Philadelphia in May 1787 and reached a quorum on May 25. With the exception of Rhode Island, all states sent delegates; fifty-five were present at one time or another. The delegates unanimously elected George Washington president of the convention and then adopted certain rules for debate. One very important decision they made was that voting would be by states and that each state would have one vote. Thus, to conduct business, delegations from seven states had to be present.

The key participants at the Philadelphia convention included George Mason and Edmund Randolph of Virginia, James Wilson and Gouverneur Morris of Pennsylvania, Charles Pinckney and Charles Cotesworth Pinckney of South Carolina, Roger Sherman and Oliver Ellsworth of Connecticut, John Dickinson of Delaware, Luther Martin of Maryland, and William Paterson of New Jersey. James Madison, an ardent proponent of a stronger general government and one of the convention's ablest minds, kept an informal journal that has provided historians with a detailed account of the proceedings.

## The Virginia Plan

Because his state had initiated the calling of the convention, Virginia's Edmund Randolph rose first to speak. He presented fifteen resolutions for the convention to consider. These resolutions, collectively known as the Virginia Plan, formed the basis of debate. The plan featured a national

▼ *This famous oil painting (c. 1856) by J. B. Stearns depicts the signing of the U.S. Constitution on September 17, 1787.*

*An unattributed painting of James Madison, known as the father of the Constitution. Madison, later the fourth U.S. president, played a key role at the Constitutional Convention, even if some of his suggestions were rejected.*

legislature with two branches. Rather than give states equal power in the legislature, as was the case under the Articles, the plan proposed that representation be linked to population. The plan also called for a national veto power over all state legislation and proposed the creation of a national executive and judiciary.

Given that the Revolution was fought, in large part, to lodge self-government in the individual states rather than in the distant British central government, Randolph's proposal for a strong general government was radical. Opponents argued that it was inconsistent with Congress's command to simply revise the Articles of Confederation and that it would destroy state sovereignty. In light of these objections, on June 15, 1787, New Jersey's William Paterson introduced an alternative plan.

## The New Jersey Plan

The central principles of Paterson's plan included expanding the powers of Congress to tax, regulate commerce, and compel disobedient states to comply with Congress's enactments. To ensure uniformity of national laws, the New Jersey Plan called for the creation of a national judiciary to hear appeals from state courts on federal matters.

After a discussion of each plan's merits, the delegates chose to continue using the Virginia Plan as the basis for discussion. The final product, however, contained principles from both plans and many compromises.

## The Three-fifths Compromise

The issue of slavery required a major compromise. Delegates from the northern states argued that slaves should not be counted in determining representation in

### ARTICLE II

At the Philadelphia convention two competing visions of the executive emerged. The more conservative delegates suggested a one-person executive with a lifetime appointment or a lengthy term. Other delegates believed this model too closely resembled the British monarchy; they proposed a plural executive with a short term of office. The result was again a compromise: Article II of the Constitution places the executive power in one person, the president, who serves a four-year term and is subject to reelection. The president's key powers under the Constitution include serving as commander in chief of the armed forces; granting pardons and reprieves; and nominating ambassadors, judges, and other officials with the advice and consent of the Senate.

The delegates considered various methods of electing a president: by the people, by state executives, by Congress, by state legislatures. Ultimately, they chose an electoral college; each state appoints electors for the specific purpose of choosing a president.

the House, because slaves could not participate in a state's political affairs. Counting slaves, they contended, would give the South an unfair advantage. Southern delegates countered that because slaves might be subject to taxation as property or on a per capita basis, they should be counted for purposes of representation. Southerners also wanted the slave population counted because additional representatives would bolster the number of those defending the institution of slavery, on which their economies depended. The compromise reached was to count each slave as three-fifths of a person. Because of objections to giving slavery constitutional standing, slaves are referred to as "other persons" in the Constitution.

**Ratification**

On September 17, 1787, the Confederation Congress submitted the proposed Constitution to the states. A great debate ensued between the Constitution's supporters, known as Federalists, and its opponents, known as Anti-Federalists. In New York the debate yielded a series of newspapers articles, written under the pen name Publius, now called the *Federalist Papers*. Actually written by Alexander Hamilton, John Jay, and James Madison, The *Federalist Papers* are the most famous and influential exposition of the Constitution ever written. Supporters of the Constitution proved victorious in all

▲ *Alexander Hamilton, pictured here in a portrait by John Trumbull, favored a more centralized government than did most of the other delegates to the Constitutional Convention, though in the* Federalist Papers *he argued in favor of its ratification.*

## ARTICLE III

Article III vests the judicial power of the United States in a Supreme Court and inferior courts created by Congress. Some delegates believed that a federal system of trial courts would be too expensive and would encroach upon the powers of the states. Others believed that a federal court system was a necessity because state judges were too dependent on state executives and legislatures. The compromise reached left the establishment of a federal court system to the discretion of Congress (it did indeed establish one).

The federal judicial power extends to certain enumerated categories, the broadest of which is all cases arising under the Constitution, federal laws, and treaties made by the United States. To permit federal judges to exercise independent judgment, the Constitution prohibits reductions in their compensation while they are serving.

thirteen states. The new government began operations in April 1789.

## Federalism

A major theme of the Constitution is federalism, which mixes elements of a confederation, in which each state retains full sovereignty; and of a national government, in which all power resides with the central government. In some areas states are fully sovereign, in some areas the national government is fully sovereign, and in some areas the two governments share power. Prior to ratification of the Constitution, many political theorists believed that such a division of power was impossible. The Constitution's federalism was a bold experiment and represents the prime American contribution to political science.

## Separation of Powers

The framers believed that an accumulation in one branch or person of all legislative, executive, and judicial powers would produce a tyrannical government. Thus, the Constitution creates three equal branches of government: Congress makes the laws, the president executes the laws, and the federal courts interpret the laws within the context of actual cases and controversies.

▲ The Federalist, *also referred to as the* Federalist Papers, *was a series of eighty-five newspaper articles written in the New York press between October 1787 and August 1788 that called for the ratification of the Constitution. Written under the pseudonym Publius, the articles were divided between Alexander Hamilton (who wrote fifty-one), James Madison (twenty-nine), and John Jay (five). This bound volume containing all the articles was printed in the late eighteenth century.*

In addition to this horizontal separation of powers, the Constitution divides power vertically—that is, between the federal and state governments—to reduce the damage from one government's abuse of power.

## CHRONOLOGY

| 1781 | 1786 | May 1787 | September 1787 | 1789 |
|---|---|---|---|---|
| The Articles of Confederation are ratified on March 1. | Delegates from five states meet in Annapolis, Maryland, to discuss matters of commerce. | Delegates from twelve American states gather in Philadelphia to amend the Articles of Confederation (instead, they draft the Constitution). | On the 17th the Confederation Congress submits the proposed Constitution to the states. | The new federal government begins operations in April, with New York City as the provisional capital. |
| **1785** Delegates from Virginia and Maryland meet at Mount Vernon, Virginia, to discuss commercial regulations. | | | | |

► *This satirical cartoon explores some of the major issues in Connecticut politics on the eve of the ratification of the U.S. Constitution. Connecticut is symbolized by a wagon sinking into the mud under its heavy load of debts and paper money. The wagon is pulled in opposite directions by two factions of the state's Council of Twelve. Connecticut's Federalists represented trading interests and supported taxes on imports, while its Anti-Federalists represented agrarian interests and were more receptive to paper-money issues. The cartoonist clearly sides with the Federalists.*

## Checks and Balances

Theoretically, the existence of multiple independent departments of government with specific functions should suffice to prevent a concentration of powers. Although the Framers believed in the separation of powers, they realized it might not prove adequate to restrain government. Accordingly, the Constitution contains checks and balances: each branch is given some authority to exercise control over the others. For example, the president can veto acts of Congress, Congress can impeach and try officials of the executive and judicial branches, and the judiciary can refuse to apply a law because it violates the Constitution.

*William J. Watkins Jr.*

### ARTICLES IV–VII

The remaining articles of the Constitution deal with such matters as the relations between states, creation of new states, and amendment and ratification of the Constitution. To take effect, the Constitution had to be ratified by representatives of the people of at least nine states meeting in separate conventions. The Framers wanted the Constitution to have the highest possible sanction, which could come only from the people of each state. Separate state conventions were also necessary because the people would be altering their state constitutions by transferring certain powers to the new federal government. Therefore, only the people of each state had the authority at once to accept the federal Constitution and implicitly alter or amend their state constitution.

**SEE ALSO**

• Articles of Confederation • Bill of Rights
• Executive System • Federalist Papers
• Hamilton, Alexander • Jay, John
• Judicial System • Legislative System
• Madison, James • Popular Sovereignty
• Slavery • State Constitutions
• Washington, George

# Continental Congresses

IN THE YEARS both immediately preceding and during the Revolutionary War, the two Continental Congresses formed the first national government of the United States. Those desirous of a strong central government were dissatisfied with the limitations on the scope and extent of these congresses' authority. Later, the inability of successive sessions of the Congress of the Articles of Confederation to settle the major political issues of the period to the satisfaction of those with a nationalist bent led ultimately to the adoption of a new system of government under the U.S. Constitution.

The Continental Congress—this designation is also commonly applied to the Congress of the Confederation, which governed the new nation while its organization was founded upon the Articles—partook of both legislative and executive functions of a central government. The congress was a unicameral body; that is to say, it contained only one chamber. The individual states maintained a significant level of independence within the congress, as each state was accorded equal representation therein; indeed, the general understanding and the intent of many of the leading figures of the Revolutionary era was that each state was a state in precisely the same sense that England and France, for example were states: they were sovereign and independent political units.

## The First Continental Congress

The First Continental Congress met in Philadelphia from September 5 to October 26, 1774, following the imposition of the Coercive Acts. Various groups wanted to bring together representatives from all of the thirteen colonies to come up with a coordinated response to British actions, much as the Stamp Act Congress had been able to do in 1765. Some fifty-six delegates attended—all the colonies except Georgia were represented—and voting was done by state, each state's representation having one vote.

*Carpenter's Hall, which hosted the First Continental Congress in 1774, is one of the historic treasures of Philadelphia and continues to attract tens of thousands of visitors annually.*

Representatives were chosen by the legislatures of the various states or by local committees; there was no popular election. Each state decided for itself the number of delegates it sent to the congress. Since most political power at the time resided with and within the states, as a rule delegates to the Continental Congress were glad to return to state politics when they were given the opportunity to do so.

**Structure and Process**

The office of president of the Congress came with little real power; it was largely an honorary or ceremonial position. Peyton Randolph of Virginia was elected the first president of the congress, among whose delegates were some of the most prominent political figures in the colonies, including Patrick Henry, Samuel Adams, and George Washington. The other main position was secretary. Charles Thomson was elected secretary in 1774 and served until 1789, through both Continental Congresses and the Congress of the Confederation.

▲ *A 1783 engraving of Charles Thomson, then secretary of the Continental Congress.*

## CHARLES THOMSON ■ 1729–1824

Charles Thomson was born on November 29, 1729, in Ireland. He came to America in 1740 and soon after became an outspoken opponent of British rule. Thomson was chosen a Pennsylvania delegate to the First Continental Congress in 1774. By a unanimous vote of the assembled representatives, he was raised to the office of secretary of the body. He was subsequently reappointed to the Second Continental Congress, and he continued to serve as the congress's official record keeper until 1789; though he received no pay for his service, he faithfully traveled with the congress as it moved from one location to another.

Along with keeping records and taking notes, Thomson oversaw the correspondence and official documents of the young nation. It is thus not surprising that in 1776 Thomson and John Hancock, who was then the congress's president, were the sole signers of the handwritten first draft of the Declaration of Independence, the draft from which copies were printed and distributed to the other delegates. Thomson is also credited with designing the Great Seal of the United States, which continues in use to this day. After 1789 Thomson devoted his time to translating the Bible from ancient Greek and Hebrew into English. He died in Montgomery County, Pennsylvania, on August 16, 1824.

## A Boycott and a Petition to the King

Once in session, the delegates to the first congress endeavored to develop a list of grievances to be sent to the British monarch. Although most resisted the idea of a complete break with the mother country, a minority of the representatives even then advocated full independence from Great Britain. Among its other actions the congress created the Continental Association, which called for a boycott of British goods and products. The boycott was devised as a means to put economic pressure on the British government to make concessions to the Americans.

On October 25, 1774, the First Continental Congress issued its formal list of grievances for redress by the king. High on the list was the Parliament's passage of the Coercive Acts—widely called the Intolerable Acts in the American colonies—the repeal of which the congress demanded. Before they adjourned the next day, the delegates voted to meet again in a year if the crown did not address the grievances.

## The Second Continental Congress

After the first congress adjourned, relations between the colonies and Great Britain worsened, and in April 1775 fighting broke out in Massachusetts, at Lexington and Concord. In response to this crisis, the Second Continental Congress was convened on May 10, 1775, in Philadelphia. All of the colonies sent representatives, although the Georgia delegation did not arrive until the end of the summer. When it was summoned, the congress was not explicitly vested with the authority to act as a government for the colonies, but it gradually assumed that role as the war progressed. Peyton Randolph was again

▲ *This 1911 oil painting by Clyde Osmer DeLand depicts delegates to the First Continental Congress (1774) filing out of a session in Philadelphia's Carpenter's Hall.*

elected president, but when ill health led him to resign, the post was given to John Hancock. Two delegates to the second congress who had not been part of the first were Thomas Jefferson and Benjamin Franklin.

Since fighting had already commenced, one of the first acts of the congress was to create the Continental Army. On June 15, 1775, George Washington was appointed the commander of the force. The congress also rejected a reconciliation plan that had been developed and proposed by the British prime minister, Lord North, and approved a statement to justify military action, the Declaration of the Causes and Necessity of Taking Up Arms (1775). In order to gain foreign support, the congress authorized the dispatch of a diplomatic mission to France in March 1776. The most important early action of the congress was the proclamation of the Declaration of

*In its justification for moving to break free of British rule, the Second Continental Congress emphasized that the original goal of the American colonists had not been independence; rather, in order to defend their rights as British subjects, they had been compelled to take up arms against the tyrannical interference of the crown.*

*We have not raised armies with ambitious designs of separating from Great-Britain, and establishing independent states. We fight not for glory or for conquest. We exhibit to mankind the remarkable spectacle of a people attacked by unprovoked enemies, without any imputation or even suspicion of offence. They [the British] boast of their privileges and civilization, and yet proffer no milder conditions than servitude or death.*

THE DECLARATION OF THE CAUSES
AND NECESSITY OF TAKING UP ARMS,
JULY 6, 1775

▼ *Frederick, Lord North and earl of Guilford, served as prime minister from 1770–1782 and was in office during most of the American Revolution. This 1792 engraving is based on a portrait of Lord North by Nathaniel Dance-Holland.*

Independence in July 1776. Mainly the work of Thomas Jefferson, the document contained a statement of political principles and a list of specific reasons to justify the separation of the colonies from Great Britain.

## The Articles of Confederation

In July 1776, soon after the Declaration of Independence was signed, a measure was introduced in the congress to create an organized but limited central government for the former colonies. The Articles of Confederation defined the role and responsibilities of the congress and the relationship of the newly created central government to the states. The Articles called for a unicameral legislature in which each state had

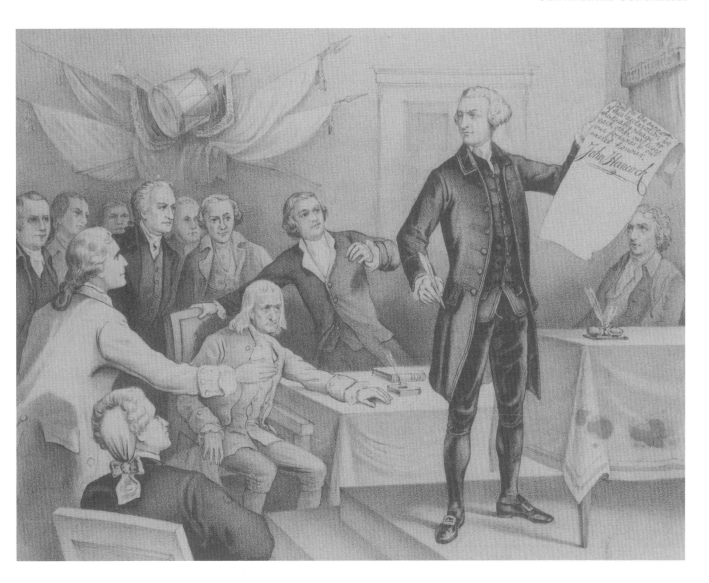

▲ *Upon the adoption of the Declaration of Independence on July 4, 1776, John Hancock, who was then the president of the Continental Congress, signed it and declared: "John Bull can read my name without spectacles and may double the reward for my head. That is my defiance." (John Bull, usually depicted as a rotund and determined man, was a personification of Great Britain.) Pictured, from left to right, are Robert Morris, Samuel Adams, Benjamin Rush, Richard Henry Lee, Charles Carroll, John Witherspoon, John Adams, John Hancock, and Edward Rutledge.*

equal representation and could veto acts of the congress. By express design most of the real power remained with the states, as may be seen from the fact that the congress was denied the power to tax or to control the currency.

## Dealing with Obstacles

The second congress faced a range of difficulties. Lacking as it did the power to tax and therefore having few resources to draw upon, it had to come up with other ways to fill the needs of the military or to provide government services. The congress could ask the states for money, of course, but could not force them to supply it, and the

states quickly showed themselves loath to comply with such requests. In an attempt to get around this obstacle, the congress resorted to the issuance of paper currency, which had little value even when issued and suffered from severe inflation as the war progressed. The congress also used bills of credit, which promised future payment by the government.

The second congress took an active role in the conduct of the Revolution. Indeed, George Washington was constantly at odds with the legislature's representatives over control of strategy and resources. Many members of the congress disagreed with his decisions and often did what they could to thwart his authority. In addition, British military actions forced the congress to move on many occasions to avoid the threat of imminent capture. In 1777 it met in Baltimore before returning to Philadelphia, only to relocate to Lancaster and then York, both also in Pennsylvania, before once again returning to Philadelphia in 1778. One result of the constant movement of the congress was that low attendance became the rule rather than the exception; at times there were only some twenty delegates in attendance.

Internal politics also took its toll on the effectiveness of the congress. By the late 1770s there were clear divisions between the southern states and the New England states (the mid-Atlantic states tended to join one faction or the other, depending on the issue). Regionally based differences existed on such issues as slavery, trade, and the scope of government.

## The End of an Era

Although the Articles of Confederation were approved on November 15, 1777, they still had to go before the state legislatures for official ratification. It was not until March 1, 1781, that the process of ratification of the Articles was finally completed. The Second Continental Congress formally adjourned in 1781, and a new body, the Congress of the Confederation, became

◀ *This replica of the Colonial Courthouse, where the Second Continental Congress met from 1777 to 1778, stands in York, Pennsylvania.*

One of the functions of the Second Continental Congress was the conduct of diplomatic affairs. In 1778 the congress instructed its representatives in France to propose a treaty of alliance with that nation. One of the main concerns of the delegates was ensuring that France not try to conquer any territory still under the control of Great Britain or part of the new United States. This concern became a formal part of the proposed treaty and was agreed to by the French.

The most Christian King [of France], shall never invade, nor under any presence attempt to possess himself of Labrador, New Britain, Nova Scotia, Acadia, Canada, Florida, nor any of the Countries, Cities, or Towns, on the Continent of North America, nor of the Islands of Newfoundland, Cape Breton, St. John's, Anticosti, nor of any other Island lying near to the said Continent, in the Seas, or in any Gulph, Bay, or River, it being the true Intent and meaning of this Treaty, that the said United States, shall have the sole, exclusive, undivided and perpetual Possession of the Countries, Cities, and Towns, on the said Continent, and of all Islands near to it, which now are, or lately were under the Jurisdiction of or Subject to the King or Crown of Great Britain, whenever they shall be united or confederated with the said United States.

JOURNALS OF THE CONTINENTAL CONGRESS, 1774–1779

◀ *This contemporary engraving depicts the French foreign minister Alexandre Gérard de Rayneval being introduced to the Continental Congress on August 6, 1778.*

the first government of the United States of America—still a federation, not yet the unitary nation that it was to become; a voluntary association of fraternally linked but entirely independent political entities.

*Tom Lansford*

**SEE ALSO**
- Articles of Confederation
- British Colonization • Coercive Acts
- Constitution of the United States
- Declaration of Independence
- Democracy in America • Elections
- Executive System • Federalist Papers
- Franklin, Benjamin
- Great Britain, Relations with
- Hancock, John
- Jefferson, Thomas • Judicial System
- Legislative System • Madison, James
- Revolutionary War • States' Rights
- Washington, George

# Cooper, James Fenimore

JAMES FENIMORE COOPER (1789–1851) is regarded as America's first major novelist. His works about the frontier impressed both domestic and European readers, and he influenced the work of subsequent writers all around the world.

James Fenimore Cooper was born on September 15, 1789, in Burlington, New Jersey, into a prominent family; his father, for whom the village of Cooperstown, New York, was named, was a judge and congressman. As a boy Cooper became fascinated with the frontier and often explored nearby native settlements. This youthful interest in the wilderness bore fruit later on.

◀ James Fenimore Cooper, the subject of this portrait by Alonzo Chappel (1828–1887), was the first American novelist to attract a large European readership.

Cooper attended Yale University but left school in 1805. After serving briefly in the navy, he resigned in 1811 and married Susan Augusta de Lancey (their daughter Susan later achieved a measure of literary fame). Cooper's family experienced a number of difficulties: four of his brothers died over a six-year period, and the family's fortunes declined precipitously during the same span. Cooper became responsible for the family's growing debt and for supporting his brothers' widows, but he had little with which to pay creditors.

**Early Literary Career**

Cooper began to write after reading a novel that was so bad that he decided he could easily write a superior one. His first novel, *Precaution*, published in 1820, was a failure with both critics and public. His second novel, *The Spy* (1821), however, was a success. Cooper soon became a prolific writer; he wrote at the rate of almost a book a year for the remainder of his life. His books were translated into French and German, and several were adapted as stage plays.

After the success of *The Spy*, Cooper began a five-novel series, *Leatherstocking Tales*, with *The Pioneers* in 1823. The tales relate the adventures of an American frontiersman named Natty Bumppo. Bumppo's appeal to readers was based on his ties to the disparate societies of the settlers and the American Indians. The character allowed Cooper to explore both cultures and highlight what he saw as the positive and negative aspects of each (though some present-day critics regard his depictions of Indians as stereotypical and overly negative). *Leatherstocking Tales* remained very popular well into the 1900s.

### The Last of the Mohicans

The second volume of the series, *The Last of the Mohicans* (1826), is Cooper's most famous novel. He uses the French and Indian Wars as a backdrop for a fictional account of a massacre of a contingent of British soldiers by the French and their Indian allies. Natty Bumppo, called Hawkeye in the novel, and his Mohican companions Chingachgook and Uncas become involved in rescuing the two daughters of a British officer from Indian captivity. Cooper's account underscores numerous differences between the American colonials and the British, differences that would lead to the Revolution. Critics of Cooper's own day praised

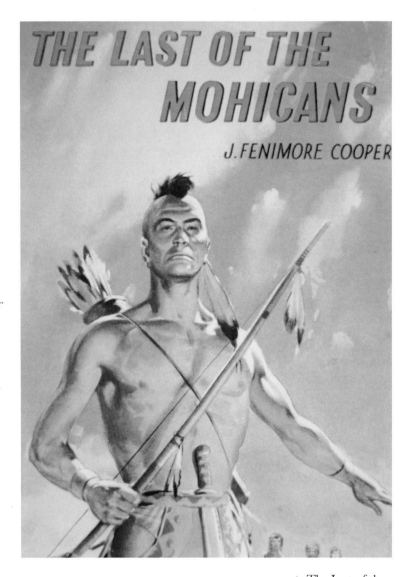

*Mohicans* as a notable achievement, and it is still considered the best American novel written to that time.

▲ The Last of the Mohicans *was Cooper's most popular book, the second in his* Leatherstocking Tales *series. This cover is taken from a 1949 edition of the book. Its somewhat romanticized depiction of an Indian warrior is not inconsistent with Cooper's own approach.*

---

**SUSAN AUGUSTA FENIMORE COOPER** ■ **1813–1894**

The daughter of James Fenimore Cooper, Susan became an author in her own right. She was born on April 17, 1813, and educated at private schools. Her father encouraged her to write, and in 1845 she produced a novel, *Elinor Wyllys*. She subsequently wrote several works of fiction and nonfiction. After her father's death, she published an edited version of his writings, *Pages and Pictures from the Writings of James Fenimore Cooper* (1861). Although a competent writer, Susan Cooper never achieved the fame of her father. In later life she devoted most of her time to philanthropy and founded a hospital and orphanage in Cooperstown. Her last book, *William West Skiles: A Sketch of Missionary Life in Valle Crucis in Western North Carolina, 1842–1862*, was published in 1890. She died on December 31, 1894.

Cooper's frontier writings provide some of the first detailed accounts of Indian lives and lifestyles and tell of the loss of territory and way of life of America's native peoples. In the introduction to **The Last of the Mohicans,** Cooper elegiacally sets the tone of the novel by describing the encroachments of the European settlers.

*The Mohicans were the possessors of the country first occupied by the Europeans in this portion of the continent. They were, consequently, the first dispossessed; and the seemingly inevitable fate of all these people, who disappear before the advances, or it might be termed the inroads, of civilization, as the verdure of their native forests falls before the nipping frosts, is represented as having already befallen them.*

▼ *This nineteenth-century engraving of a scene from* The Last of the Mohicans *depicts Natty Bumppo (Hawkeye) and his companion Chingachgook.*

### Later Achievements

Cooper's fame and family connections led to his appointment as the U.S. consul in Lyon, France, where he lived from 1826 to 1833. While there he continued writing and became popular with European readers. When he returned to America, he wrote a number of works critical of contemporary politics and society. Some of them were so vitriolic that they led to charges of libel. Though he avoided conviction, Cooper spent a good deal of time and money in court over the next decade.

Throughout this difficult period Cooper never ceased to write. Together, the trials and the pace at which he worked left him emotionally and physically drained. By the mid-1840s his health was in serious decline; nevertheless, his desire to write was unflagging. The increasing interest in experimentation evident in his later works culminated in a novel about the supernatural, *The Crater; or, Vulcan's Peak,* in 1847. Cooper died in Cooperstown on September 14, 1851.

*Tom Lansford*

SEE ALSO
• British Colonization • Colonial Wars
• Literature • Native Americans
• Revolutionary War

# Crockett, David

DAVID CROCKETT (1786–1836) was a frontiersman and statesman who became legendary in his own time. He was known as a defender of the liberty of the common citizen, and his bravery at the Battle of the Alamo cemented his place in American history.

David Crockett (he is now popularly called Davy) was born in a small cabin in eastern Tennessee's mountainous Greene County on August 17, 1786, the fifth of nine children of John and Rebecca Crockett. Young Davy accompanied cattle drives and wagon trains and developed hunting, trapping, shooting, and fighting skills as he did. At age twenty he married Mary Finley, called Polly, who bore him two sons.

During the Creek Indian War (1813–1814), Crockett served under Andrew Jackson as a scout, spy, and sergeant (in 1777 Creeks had killed Crockett's grandfather, also named David, along with two dozen other settlers in eastern Tennessee). In 1815 Polly Crockett died after giving birth to a daughter, Margaret; David soon married Elizabeth Patton, a widow with two children.

## Buckskin Congressman

In 1818 Crockett was appointed town commissioner of Lawrenceburg, Tennessee, and colonel of the Fifty-seventh Militia. Three years later he ran for a seat in the Tennessee state legislature and won. A plainspoken man with little education, Crockett believed in limited, representative government and in preserving the rights of squatters in frontier territories. After moving to western Tennessee in 1822, he was elected to another term in the legislature, this time to represent the interests of the settlers of the area he now called home.

▲ *This portrait by J. G. Chapman (1808–1889) depicts Crockett as the great frontiersman, hat and rifle in hand. Crockett also served in the Tennessee legislature and in the U.S. Congress.*

Crockett ran for a seat in the U.S. Congress in 1827 as a man of the people and won. In cultivating his image as an honest frontiersman, he was associated early on with Andrew Jackson, a fellow Tennessean and his former militia commander.

However, after Crockett's reelection in 1829, conflicts with Jackson (now president) over the latter's refusal to grant squatters the right to purchase the property on which they lived led Crockett to a public split with Old Hickory. After this break leaders of the Whigs began to court Crockett, regaling him with speeches, parties, and awards. They sent him on a tour of the northeastern states during which he denounced Jackson and the Democrats' policies.

## Glory at the Alamo

Having lost his seat in the 1835 election, Crockett set out on November 1 of that year for Texas, where revolution was in the

*During Crockett's time in the House of Representatives, Congress was to decide on a bill that would grant the widow of a U.S. naval officer $20,000. Crockett, rising in opposition, argued that to dispense such charity from the U.S. Treasury, while noble, would be unconstitutional. Instead, he invited his fellow congressmen to join him in donating a week's pay to help the woman. After Crockett's oration the bill was defeated. He later opined about the freedom of congressmen in dispensing other people's money.*

There are in that House many very wealthy men—men who think nothing of spending a week's pay, or a dozen of them, for a dinner or a wine party when they have something to accomplish by it. Some of those same men made beautiful speeches upon the great debt of gratitude which the country owed the deceased—a debt which could not be paid by money—and the insignificance and worthlessness of money, particularly so insignificant a sum as $20,000 when weighed against the honor of the nation. Yet not one of them responded to my proposition. Money with them is nothing but trash when it is to come out of the people. But it is the one great thing for which most of them are striving, and many of them sacrifice honor, integrity, and justice to obtain it.

QUOTED IN EDWARD SYLVESTER ELLIS, *THE LIFE OF COLONEL DAVID CROCKETT*

◀ *Crockett's bravery at the Alamo, where he perished in early 1836, assured him an honored place in American history. The Battle of the Alamo has been the subject of countless television, documentary, and motion picture treatments.*

▶ *A portrait of Crockett by John Neagle (1796–1865).*

air. He looked to settle there with his family and serve in the new government. Upon arriving in Texas and learning of the impending battle in San Antonio de Bexar, he led a dozen Tennessee volunteers to the Alamo, a mission fortified with around two hundred Texans, on February 8, 1836. Colonel Travis offered to share his command with the legendary frontiersman, but Crockett insisted on being a mere "high private," perched on the walls with his Tennessee boys. Already a hero in the eyes of many men in the doomed fortress, he entertained them with his fiddle when he was not picking off Mexicans from his post.

During the bloody siege that began on February 23, Crockett fought valiantly. The Alamo fell on March 6; Crockett killed an opponent with his sword before being run through with bayonets. Most reliable accounts bear witness to his death near the battle's end, but a few recent historians argue that Crockett survived the battle and was executed as a prisoner of war. Their theory is based on the "memoir" of a Mexican lieutenant, José Enrique de la Peña, that most scholars consider a forgery. More reliable is the eyewitness account of Susanna Dickinson—her husband, an artillery officer, had perished in the fray—who wrote that, before the Mexican commander Santa Anna arrived and demanded to be shown the bodies of the important men, she saw Colonel Crockett, "his peculiar cap by his side . . . lying dead and mutilated" outside the chapel door. Several journal entries by Mexican officers confirm this version of events.

*Aaron D. Wolf*

*Crockett's presence on the walls of the mission fortress encouraged the Alamo's defenders, and the long rifles and marksmanship of Crockett and his Tennessee volunteers struck fear into the hearts of the attacking Mexicans. A member of Santa Anna's force described the scene in his journal.*

*A tall man, with flowing hair, was seen firing from the same place on the parapet during the entire siege. He wore a buckskin suit and a cap all of a pattern entirely different from those worn by his comrades. This man would kneel or lie down behind the low parapet, rest his long gun and fire, and we all learned to keep at a good distance when he was seen to make ready to shoot. He rarely missed his mark, and when he fired he always rose to his feet and calmly reloaded his gun seemingly indifferent to the shots fired at him by our men. . . . This man I later learned was known as "Kwockey."*

JOURNAL OF DON RAFAEL SALDAÑA

SEE ALSO
• Alamo, Battle of the • Jackson, Andrew
• Mexico, Relations with • Texas

# Cuffe, Paul

**PAUL CUFFE (1759–1817)** was a prominent African American who used his wealth to fight slavery and to improve the lot of other black people. He later supported efforts to resettle freedmen in Africa.

Paul Cuffe was born on January 17, 1759, on Cuttyhunk Island, Massachusetts, the youngest of ten children. His father was a former slave who had purchased his freedom, and his mother was an American Indian. Education was important to his parents, who taught their children reading, writing, and arithmetic. After his father died, Cuffe, then sixteen, began serving on merchant and whaling ships, where he learned navigation and seamanship. He also became a devout Quaker.

**A Revolutionary and an Entrepreneur**

Cuffe was a staunch supporter of the Revolutionary cause. He hoped that independence would lead to greater freedom and equality for African Americans. During the American Revolution, Cuffe and his brother built their own vessel and began transporting goods through the British naval blockade. The voyages were dangerous—the ships faced attack by both British naval vessels and pirate ships. Cuffe was once briefly captured by the British (who released him) and on several occasions had to outrun pirates.

The voyages were also extremely profitable. Cuffe used the profits to build a shipyard to produce more ships; eventually he was the owner of one of the largest shipping firms in New England and was one of the wealthiest men in America. He employed many African Americans in his company and consistently tried to improve the economic status of the free black population in Massachusetts.

PAUL CUFFE

CAPTAIN

1812.

ENGRAVED FOR ABRM. L. PENNOCK, BY MASON & MAAS.

◀ *This silhouette of Paul Cuffe (whose surname was sometimes spelled Cuffee) sits above a ship docked in a tropical region—possibly Sierra Leone, where Cuffe sought to resettle freed American slaves.*

## AN APPEAL TO PRESIDENT MADISON

Paul Cuffe was the kind of man who bridled at taking no for an answer. In 1812, pursuant to a local tax collector's complaint, one of his ships was refused clearance to leave Norfolk, Virginia, because its crew was black. Cuffe appealed the harbormaster's decision directly to President James Madison. The president agreed to meet face-to-face with Cuffe, who convinced Madison, a native Virginian, of the injustice of the seizure of his ship. Madison ordered the tax collector at Norfolk to release Cuffe's vessel.

### A Champion of Voting Rights

In 1780 Cuffe launched an effort to persuade the legislature of Massachusetts to give free black people the right to vote. He based his argument on the broader themes of the Revolution, including the unfairness of taxation without representation—African Americans were taxed but could not vote or elect members to the county council. His efforts were successful, and the right to vote was granted to blacks in Massachusetts in 1783.

After the Revolution, Cuffe settled in Westport, Connecticut. He bought a large farm and became increasingly involved in the surrounding Quaker community. He donated money to Quaker and other charities. He even paid to construct a school for the Westport area and a new meeting-house for the local Quaker community.

### Resettlement Movement

In spite of his wealth and success, Cuffe continued to feel the sting of racial discrimination. In addition, he was especially disappointed that black Americans had not been able to gain greater economic or political freedom after the Revolution. By the early 1800s Cuffe had grown interested in the notion of resettlement in West Africa. Since African Americans were not going to

be treated fairly in the new United States, he reasoned, they needed their own land. Cuffe also thought his financial resources could turn West Africa into a prosperous center of trade and industry. He hoped to undermine the slave trade at its source by creating strong, independent, African-ruled states.

Cuffe spent four years planning and gathering support for resettlement. He even traveled to Africa to explore the region in 1811. Over the next few years, Cuffe worked to gain allies for his idea, but the War of 1812 slowed his efforts. His repeated petitions to the U.S. government for political and financial backing were rebuffed. On December 10, 1815, he set sail with thirty-eight settlers for Sierra Leone, a colony the British had established for freed slaves and other black Americans that had fought on their side during the American Revolution.

Once in Sierra Leone, Cuffe again encountered resistance, this time from British officials and local merchants. Nevertheless, he remained enthusiastic about his project, and his settlement initially prospered, mainly because of his financial support. Cuffe returned to America to enlist more settlers, but his health began to fail. Before he could make

[Africans have] declined the practice of selling [members of] their own tribe; but notwithstanding this, they continue to sell those of other tribes, and thought it hard that the traffic in slaves should be abolished, as they were made poor in consequence thereof. As they themselves were not willing to submit to the bonds of slavery, I endeavored to hold this out as a light to convince them of their error. But the prejudice of education had taken too firm hold of their minds to admit of much effect from reason on this subject.

PAUL CUFFE, *A BRIEF ACCOUNT OF THE SETTLEMENT AND PRESENT SITUATION OF THE COLONY OF SIERRA LEONE*

▲ In 1816 Cuffe brought thirty-eight freed slaves to Freetown, Sierra Leone, for voluntary resettlement. He died the following year before he could pursue the project further.

further progress on his resettlement initiative, however, Cuffe died in Westport on September 9, 1817. In 1824 Cuffe's efforts bore fruit with the establishment of Liberia as an independent colony for freed American slaves.

*Tom Lansford*

SEE ALSO
• Abolitionism • Madison, James
• New England Colonies • Race Relations
• Religion and Religious Movements
• Revolutionary War • Slavery
• War of 1812

# Custer, George Armstrong

ALTHOUGH HE IS NOW best known for his catastrophic defeat at the hands of a vast Sioux-led coalition of warros at the Battle of the Little Bighorn in 1876, George Armstrong Custer (1839–1876) was in his own day a controversial and flamboyant cavalry commander whose widely observed career had its start with service in the Union army during the Civil War.

George Armstrong Custer was born in New Rumley, Ohio, and was raised in Monroe, Michigan. He was admitted to the U.S. Military Academy at West Point, and he graduated at the bottom of his class in 1861. His military career also started poorly. Several days after graduation he failed to stop a fight between two West Point cadets. Although he was court-martialed and convicted for this failure to act, he was spared punishment because of the desperate need for officers in 1861 to occupy positions of command in the rapidly expanding Union army during this, the first year of the Civil War.

## A Dashing Figure on the Battlefield

Despite the poor start to his military career, Custer redeemed himself during the Civil War through his bravery and aggressive leadership, primarily as a cavalry commander. He also established a reputation as a flamboyant figure during the war, in part because of his frequent acts of reckless courage, in part because he had taken to wearing a crimson necktie and a black velvet coat trimmed with gold lace.

Custer participated in all but one of the Army of the Potomac's major campaigns during the war. He started out as a cavalry lieutenant and finished as a major general— a rank bestowed upon him during the final campaign of the war. In recognition of his

contributions to the war effort, General Philip Sheridan gave Custer the table on which the Confederate commander, General Robert E. Lee, surrendered at Appomattox Court House.

◀ A hand-colored photograph of Major General George Armstrong Custer, who earned praise for his service in the Civil War but is remembered for his disastrous defeat at the Battle of the Little Bighorn in 1876.

### Western Frontier

After the conclusion of the Civil War, Custer remained in the U.S. Army and was appointed lieutenant colonel of the Seventh Cavalry Regiment in July 1866 (his Civil War rank of major general was a temporary one). In 1867 and 1868, Custer's unit was posted to the western frontier at Fort Riley, Kansas, from where it participated in campaigns against the Cheyenne Indian tribe, including the Battle of the Washita River (1868).

### Battle of the Little Bighorn

In 1873 Custer was transferred to the Northern Plains, where he led an expedition of 1,200 men into the Black Hills of South Dakota against several Native American nations. In 1876, accompanied by three columns of troops, he participated in a campaign to trap the Lakota, Cheyenne, and Arapaho tribes. Custer's impatience, however, undermined the coordination of the assault. He pushed forward much more quickly than the plans called for, and then on the morning of June 25, 1876, he launched a foolhardy attack on an Indian village, unaware that one of the other columns had been forced to retreat. To ensure that he would catch as many Indians as possible, he split his column into three groups.

In a quick turn of events, it was Custer's own troops that needed to escape. Thousands of Indian warriors pushed Custer's unit onto a ridge parallel to the Little Bighorn ridge. Custer and every one of his officers and enlisted men—some 210 men in all—perished on that ridgeline. The defeat, now known as the Battle of the Little Bighorn, remains one of the worst in the history of the U.S. Army.

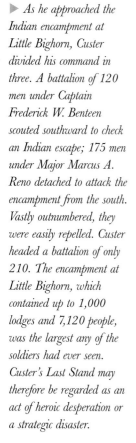

▶ *As he approached the Indian encampment at Little Bighorn, Custer divided his command in three. A battalion of 120 men under Captain Frederick W. Benteen scouted southward to check an Indian escape; 175 men under Major Marcus A. Reno detached to attack the encampment from the south. Vastly outnumbered, they were easily repelled. Custer headed a battalion of only 210. The encampment at Little Bighorn, which contained up to 1,000 lodges and 7,120 people, was the largest any of the soldiers had ever seen. Custer's Last Stand may therefore be regarded as an act of heroic desperation or a strategic disaster.*

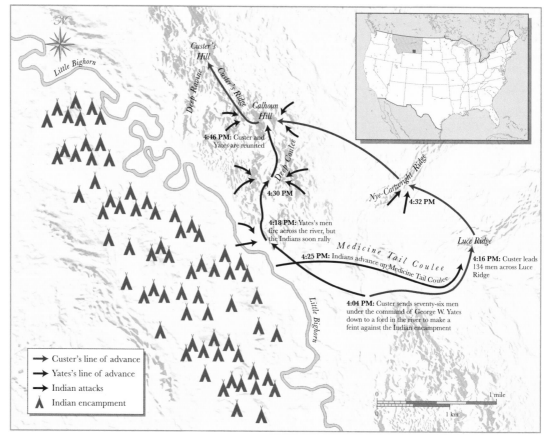

4:46 PM: Custer and Yates are reunited

4:30 PM

4:32 PM

4:18 PM: Yates's men fire across the river, but the Indians soon rally

4:25 PM: Indians advance up Medicine Tail Coulee

4:16 PM: Custer leads 134 men across Luce Ridge

4:04 PM: Custer sends seventy-six men under the command of George W. Yates down to a ford in the river to make a feint against the Indian encampment

Custer's Hill
Little Bighorn
Deep Ravine
Custer's Ridge
Calhoun Hill
Deep Coulee
Nye-Cartwright Ridge
Luce Ridge
Medicine Tail Coulee
Little Bighorn

→ Custer's line of advance
→ Yates's line of advance
→ Indian attacks
▲ Indian encampment

0   1 mile
0   1 km

◀ *Feodor Fuchs's color lithograph* Custer's Last Charge *(1876) depicts the fateful battle between Custer's troops and the Indians who defeated him. It is not entirely obvious from this painting that the battle will go down in history as one of the U.S. Army's worst losses.*

*This newspaper account, written shortly after the Battle of the Little Bighorn, reveals that contemporaries were aware of Custer's strengths and weaknesses as a commander.*

*General Custer had personal and soldierly traits which commended him to the people. He was an officer who did not know the word fear, and, as is often the case with soldiers of this stamp, he was reckless, hasty, and impulsive, preferring to make a dare-devil rush and take risks rather than to move slower and with more certainty. He was a brave, brilliant soldier, handsome and dashing, with all the attributes to make him beloved of women and admired of men; but these qualities, however admirable they may be should not blind our eyes to the fact that it was his own madcap haste, rashness, and love of fame that cost him his own life, and cost the service the loss of many brave officers and gallant men. They drew him into an ambuscaded ravine. . . . In this instance three hundred troops were instantly surrounded by 3,000 Indians, and the fatal ravine became a slaughter-pen from which few escaped. . . . No account seems to have been taken of numbers, of the leadership of the Sioux, of their record of courage and military skill.*

CHICAGO TRIBUNE, JULY 4, 1876

## Posterity's Judgment

Despite the fact that Custer's bravado and deficiencies of character were well known to his contemporaries, it was at least a generation before he ceased to be hailed as a hero and a martyr to the cause of westward expansion. No small part of this popular verdict stemmed from a chivalrous desire to spare his widow the additional pain of seeing her dead husband charged with imprudence or even incompetence. With the passage of time, however, a juster estimation of the man and his actions has become the norm.

*Eric Nelson*

**SEE ALSO**
• Armed Forces and Military Campaigns
• Civil War • Indian Treaties
• Indian Wars • Native Americans

# Davis, Jefferson

THE PRESIDENT of the Confederate States of America during the Civil War, Jefferson Davis (1808–1889), was an accomplished soldier, politician, and statesman. Deprived of the right to hold public office after the war, Davis was finally restored to full citizenship in 1978 by an act of Congress.

Jefferson Davis was born on June 3, 1808, in Christian County, Kentucky, the youngest of the ten children of Samuel Emory Davis and Jane Cook Davis. He was named for his father's hero, Thomas Jefferson. Even though he was a Baptist, Davis at the age of seven began receiving an education at a Catholic school in Washington County, Kentucky. By the age of ten, he was attending Jefferson College in Washington, Mississippi; later, he attended Transylvania University in Lexington, Kentucky. At sixteen Davis entered the U.S. Military Academy at West Point, New York.

### Early Military Career

Upon graduating from West Point in 1828, Davis was commissioned a second lieutenant. Posted to Wisconsin for the next four years, he first saw combat in the Black Hawk War of 1832. Black Hawk, a Sauk Indian chief, was unhappy with the terms of a treaty that his tribe had negotiated with the U.S. government in 1804. After Black Hawk was captured, Davis was chosen by his commander, the future U.S. president Zachary Taylor, to escort the chief to the prison where he was to be held. Black Hawk would later write glowingly of his

▶ *Following a distinguished military and political career, Jefferson Davis, the subject of this nineteenth-century portrait by Christian F. Schwerdt, became president of the Confederate States of America.*

treatment by Davis and call him a "good and brave young chief."

Two years later, in 1834, Taylor refused Davis's request to marry his daughter, Sarah Knox Taylor. Davis resigned his commission and married the sixteen-year-old Sarah anyway. She died three months later from malaria, a disease that Davis had contracted as well. Davis returned to Mississippi, where his family had moved when he was a young child, and started a plantation on land given to him by his brother Joseph, who, twenty-three years older than Davis, had become essentially a second father to him after the death of their father in 1824.

## From Politics to War

By 1843 Davis had decided to run for public office. After an unsuccessful bid for a seat in the Mississippi House of Representatives, he won election to the U.S. House of Representatives in 1844. A week before he took office in 1845, Davis married Varina Howell, who would bear him six children and outlive her husband by sixteen years.

Davis's career as a congressman was short lived. When the Mexican War was declared in 1846, he resigned his seat and, over his wife's objection, accepted a commission as a colonel in the First Mississippi Regiment. Despite her concerns, he would return from the war a hero. He even won back the respect of Zachary Taylor, who told him, "My daughter, sir, was a better judge of men than I was."

▲ *This 1870 oil-on-canvas portrait of Black Hawk, the Native American chief who for a time was Jefferson Davis's prisoner, was painted by Homer Henderson.*

---

*The prospect of her husband's volunteering to fight in the Mexican War was hard on the young Varina Davis, barely twenty and married for just over one year. As Jefferson Davis prepared to take command of the First Mississippi Regiment, Varina wrote to her mother on June 6, 1846.*

*Today I am so miserable I feel as if I could lay down my life to be near to you and Father. It has been a struggle between Jeff and me, which should overcome the other in this matter of his volunteering, and though it was carried on in love between us, it is not the less bitter. Jeff promised me he would not volunteer, but he could not help it I suppose. . . . I found out last night accidentally that he had committed himself about going. I have cried until I am stupid. . . . Jeff thinks there is something the matter with me, but I know there is not. . . . Jeff is such a dear good fellow. I might quarrel a month and he would not get mad.*

QUOTED IN HUDSON STRODE, *JEFFERSON DAVIS: PRIVATE LETTERS, 1823–1889*

*This studio photograph of Jefferson Davis's wife, born Varina Howell (1826–1905), was taken during the 1860s.*

**Back to Politics**

Davis was appointed a U.S. senator from Mississippi in the fall of 1847 to fill out the term of Senator Jesse Speight, who had died. Elected in his own right to the same seat in 1850, Davis resigned in September 1851 to run for governor of Mississippi, the centerpiece of his campaign being opposition to the Compromise of 1850. After being defeated, he poured his efforts into Franklin Pierce's successful 1852 presidential campaign; Pierce appointed Davis secretary of war.

In 1856 Davis was again elected to the U.S. Senate, where he consistently opposed the growing sentiment in the southern states for secession. After Abraham Lincoln was elected president in 1860 and Mississippi seceded on January 21, 1861, Davis resigned from the Senate to defend his home state. On February 18 he was inaugurated the provisional president of the Confederate States of America (CSA).

**The Civil War**

Davis moved quickly to try to broker a peace with the government in Washington, DC. At the same time, however, he prepared for war. In May 1861, shortly after war broke out, the Confederacy established its government in Richmond, and Davis and his family took up residence there.

Davis was elected CSA president in November 1861 and would hold that office for the rest of the war. Unlike his counterpart, Lincoln, who planned and directed the Union effort but left most of the strictly military decisions to his generals, Davis actively formulated the Confederate military campaign. Realizing that the Confederacy was at a disadvantage in matériel and manpower, Davis sought to fight a mainly defensive war toward the goal of securing independence. He did, however, allow General Robert E. Lee, whom he appointed as commander of the Army of Northern Virginia in June 1862, to attempt an invasion of Pennsylvania in mid-1863. After the Confederate defeat at Gettysburg, Davis refused to accept Lee's resignation, and he ultimately appointed Lee general in chief on January 31, 1865. Ten weeks later Lee would surrender to the Union general Ulysses S. Grant near the village of Appomattox Court House, Virginia. Davis, having fled Richmond for Greensboro, North Carolina, was heading to Mississippi when he was captured on May 10, 1865, at Irwinville, Georgia.

## JEFFERSON DAVIS AND THE CATHOLIC CHURCH

During the Civil War, Davis initiated a correspondence with Pope Pius IX, who had suffered through a similar war in Italy. On September 23, 1863, Davis wrote to Pius, "I have read with emotion the terms in which you are pleased to express the deep sorrow with which you regard the slaughter, ruin, and devastation consequent on the war now waged by the Government of the United States against the States and people over which I have been chosen to preside. . . ." Pius's response of December 3, 1863, praised Davis's expressed desire for peace: "Oh, that the other people also of the States and their rulers, considering seriously how cruel and how deplorable is this internecine war, would receive and embrace the counsels of peace and tranquillity."

During Davis's postwar imprisonment Pius sent him a picture of himself inscribed with the Gospel verse, "Come unto me, all ye who are weary and heavy laden, and I will give you rest." He also sent Davis a crown of thorns, symbolic of the suffering of Jesus Christ, which Pius himself had woven. The crown can still be seen at the Confederate Civil War Museum in New Orleans, Louisiana.

◄ *Following the Civil War, Pope Pius IX (reigned 1846–1878) sent an imprisoned Davis a crown of thorns he had made with his own hands. Earlier, in 1863, in a reply to a letter from Davis, the pope (pictured here in a photograph taken around 1865) had used the salutation "illustrious and honorable president." Some interpreted this use of Davis's political title to be an implicit act of diplomatic recognition of the Confederacy by the Vatican, though Confederate Secretary of State Judah Benjamin considered it an insignificant formality.*

▲ *Jefferson Davis's funeral procession along the streets of New Orleans in 1889. "He has always been the hero of his people–their best beloved," wrote the* Times-Democrat.

## A MAN OF PRINCIPLE TO THE END

Although deprived of the ability to hold federal office by the Fourteenth Amendment, Jefferson Davis never applied for a pardon, even though President Andrew Johnson several times hinted that he would grant one if asked. Davis firmly believed he had done nothing wrong–though he had opposed secession on practical grounds, he was convinced of its constitutionality–and he would not make a request that would imply a betrayal of his principles. In 1978 President Jimmy Carter signed a bill posthumously restoring Davis to the full rights of citizenship.

## Life after the War

Davis spent the next two years in confinement awaiting trial on charges of treason. The conditions in the prison at Fort Monroe, Virginia, were abominable, and even some northern supporters of the war, Horace Greeley and Cornelius Vanderbilt among them, began believing that the government, hoping to avoid a trial (which many thought Davis would win), wanted Davis to die in prison. He was released in 1867, and his indictment was dropped in February 1869 after President Andrew Johnson proclaimed an amnesty covering all who had participated in military action against the U.S. government.

Davis lived another twenty years, during which he wrote two books defending the Confederacy and the right of states to secede; he also traveled throughout Europe. Davis died on December 6, 1889, in New Orleans, Louisiana, and was temporarily buried there. Three years later his body was moved to Richmond, Virginia, where a funeral, attended by as many as 200,000 people, was held.

*Scott P. Richert*

SEE ALSO
- Amendments, Post–Civil War
- Armed Forces and Military Campaigns
- Civil War • Compromise of 1850
- Confederate States of America
- Constitution of the United States
- Grant, Ulysses • Greeley, Horace
- Indian Treaties • Indian Wars
- Jefferson, Thomas • Johnson, Andrew
- Lee, Robert E. • Lincoln, Abraham
- Medicine, Disease, and Epidemics
- Mexican War • Pierce, Franklin
- Secession • States' Rights
- Taylor, Zachary • Vanderbilt, Cornelius

# Declaration of Independence

IN THE DECLARATION OF INDEPENDENCE, the thirteen American colonies formally pronounced themselves independent of Great Britain. The document is best known to many for the statement "all men are created equal." Yet since the declaration describes not only the circumstances but also the colonial vision of effective government, its importance as a guide to acquiring a clear picture of the people and place that produced it extends well beyond the ideas of equality and independence.

The Declaration of Independence was the result not of an isolated event but rather of a long series of abuses of power. Encapsulating as it does a history of dissatisfaction, the Declaration needs to be examined within the historical, political, and intellectual context of colonial America to be rightly understood.

## Mercantilism and Its Discontents

Frustration with British rule was widespread in colonial America of the 1760s and 1770s. Two of the best-known causes of this frustration were the Stamp Act of 1765 and the series of laws, some of which dated from the 1660s, known collectively as the Navigation Acts. Americans viewed as burdensome the taxes and restrictive trade practices placed on the colonies by a distant government in which they had no representation. The Stamp Act required the purchase of an official stamp from British officials for all legal documents, newspapers, and pamphlets. The Navigation Acts, which required all trade with the colonies, import or export, to pass through Great Britain, created a major burden for the economic growth of the colonies.

By the 1770s resentment of these and similar policies imposed by the British

▲ *The original Declaration of Independence, which declared the American colonies' independence from Great Britain, is on view at the National Archives in Washington, DC.*

authorities often resulted in public protests by average citizens. The most famous of these protests was the Boston Tea Party. In December 1773 colonists, disguised as

▲ *An unattributed painting of the Boston Tea Party, a protest against British trade and taxation policies. The perceived harshness of the British response did much to unite the colonies in opposition to British rule.*

Mohawk Indians (though no one was fooled by the disguise), destroyed more than three hundred crates of tea on board three merchant ships in Boston harbor to protest what they considered the unfair policy of the British government with regard to the importation of tea. Whatever the merits of this case or others, the sequence of protests followed by legislative reaction followed by fresh protests eventually led to organized armed conflict, first at Lexington and Concord in May 1775 and then at Bunker Hill in June. Although war was not yet officially declared, it was clear to many even at the time that the fight for independence had begun with those conflicts.

### *Common Sense* Prevails

In colonial America distribution of pamphlets was a popular way to help shape public opinion. Fueling the colonists' discontent, numerous pamphlets began to voice opposition to the varied political and economic aspects of British colonial rule. The most famous of the pamphlets was *Common Sense*. Written by Thomas Paine, a recent English immigrant, and published in January 1776, it anticipated the words of the Declaration of Independence by urging equality among individuals and consent of the governed as the only bases of legitimate government; it also called for independence from the British. The immediate and widespread popularity of Paine's pamphlet ensured that independence would be a major topic of debate in the American colonies, from New England to Georgia.

*It was Thomas Paine's aim to move the matter of American independence from a topic of controversy to a common cause.*

*Let the names of Whig and Tory be extinct; and let none other be heard among us, than those of a good citizen, an open and resolute friend, and a virtuous supporter of the rights of mankind, and the free and independent states of America.*

APPENDIX TO THE THIRD EDITION

OF *COMMON SENSE*

**COMMON SENSE;**

ADDRESSED TO THE

**INHABITANTS**

OF

**A M E R I C A,**

On the following interesting

**S U B J E C T S.**

I. Of the Origin and Design of Government in general, with concise Remarks on the English Constitution.

II. Of Monarchy and Hereditary Succession.

III. Thoughts on the present State of American Affairs.

IV. Of the present Ability of America, with some miscellaneous Reflections.

A NEW EDITION, with several Additions in the Body of the Work. To which is added an APPENDIX; together with an Address to the People called QUAKERS.

N. B. The New Addition here given increases the Work upwards of one Third.

Man knows no Master save creating HEAVEN,
Or those whom Choice and common Good ordain.
THOMSON.

*The title page to Thomas Paine's* Common Sense, *which played an important role in persuading the colonists to opt for independence from Britain. George Washington himself observed and commented on the pamphlet's effects on public opinion.*

## The Continental Congress and the Lee Resolution

The growing desire for total independence soon moved from discussions among individual citizens to the colonial assemblies and the Continental Congress. The Second Continental Congress convened in Philadelphia on May 10, 1776, and one of its first actions was to authorize all thirteen colonies to form governments independent of Great Britain (and of one another). On May 14 Rhode Island became the first colony to announce its independence. The call for independence was soon to be heard throughout the colonies, but it was Virginia that unified the movement.

On May 15, 1776, the leaders of the Virginia legislature, the House of Burgesses, met in Williamsburg not only to declare their state's independence from British rule but also to instruct the delegation to the Second Continental Congress to introduce a motion declaring independence for all thirteen colonies. On June 7, 1776, Richard Henry Lee, the head of Virginia's congressional delegation, introduced what is now known as the Lee Resolution, which stated that the American colonies "are, and of right ought to be, free and independent states" and that all political connections with Great Britain should be dissolved.

## Debates and a Draft

The Continental Congress responded on June 11 by appointing a committee to rewrite the Lee Resolution in the form of a declaration of independence for the thirteen colonies. The committee was composed of John Adams of Massachusetts, Benjamin Franklin of Pennsylvania, Thomas Jefferson of Virginia, Robert Livingston of New York, and Roger Sherman of Connecticut. Owing largely to his formidable reputation as both an intellectual eminence and an accomplished writer, Thomas Jefferson was assigned the task of drafting the document declaring the independence of the American colonies.

Jefferson, having worked alone, submitted his draft to the congress on July 1, and after several days of debate and revision, the Second Continental Congress approved Jefferson's declaration and ordered a limited printing of the document. Contrary to popular belief, not all fifty-six members of the congress joined John Hancock, the president of the body, when he signed the declaration on July 4. The official signing actually took place on August 2, 1776, and fearing retaliation by the British, the congress did not authorize an official printing of the Declaration of Independence, one that listed all of the signers, until January 18, 1777, following the defeat of the British armies at Trenton and Princeton, when the odds of overall victory seemed markedly improved.

It is important to note that the original document did not declare the independence of one country, the United States of America; rather, it declared the independence of "the thirteen united States of America." That is to say, each state was declaring itself a sovereign and independent nation. Not until the ratification of the Constitution in 1789 was the United States of America reconstituted as a single nation, or more accurately, a confederation of sovereign states.

## The Influence of the Enlightenment

In drafting the Declaration, Thomas Jefferson was influenced not only by the historical and political currents of the day but also by the intellectual and social phenomenon known as the Enlightenment.

▼ *Contrary to popular opinon, John Trumbull's painting* Declaration of Independence *(1817–1819), a detail of which is reproduced below, depicts not the signing of the declaration but rather Congress's reception of the work of the five-member drafting committee.*

*The intellectual attitudes both expressed and implied in the Declaration of Independence were not uncommon among the colonists. Indeed, late in his life Thomas Jefferson wrote that his aim had been*

*. . . not to find out new principles, or new arguments, never before thought of, not merely to say things which had never been said before; but to place before mankind the common sense of the subject, in terms so plain and firm as to command their assent.*

LETTER TO RICHARD HENRY LEE, MAY 8, 1825

▲ *Built in the mid-1700s, Philadelphia's Independence Hall, officially known as the Pennsylvania State House, was the site of the adoption of the Declaration of Independence in 1776. In 1787, the U.S. Constitution was drafted and signed there as well.*

The Enlightenment was the product of an attempt by philosophers to develop a series of "laws" for the social and political world similar to the laws of nature that the great figures of the seventeenth-century scientific revolution—Galileo, Johannes Kepler, René Descartes, and above all, Isaac Newton—had discovered. Applying the observational and analytical tools of the new scientific method to human nature, social and political thinkers sought to arrive at broadly applicable laws in their own sphere of interest: human societies. Their goal was to find a social law as universal as the law of gravity, a law that would apply to all individuals and all societies.

They found their answer in a new version of an old concept, the idea of natural law (or God's law, as Enlightenment writers often term it), a law whose perception distinguishes human beings from other creatures. These thinkers believed that the distinguishing human feature was reason and that individuals could discover the laws of nature by exercising their reason. (Although Enlightenment writers often write of God and of natural law as God's law, the God to which they refer is a natural force for good rather than a biblical or Christian God. Religion in the traditional sense was not necessary in Enlightenment thinking.) Reason and reason alone allowed individuals to discover natural law and to then properly order not only themselves but also society. On the basis of the assumption that both human nature and reason were universal, it was assumed that the resulting "enlightened" organization of social and political affairs would also be universal.

## A Product of Its Times

Enlightenment-influenced thinking had had a tremendous impact in colonial America, and Thomas Jefferson was considered one of its major exponents, as was Thomas Paine, the author of *Common Sense*. Jefferson once wrote that the ideas he had expressed in the declaration were not new but simply a restatement of ideas current in the colonies. His application of the laws of nature to the political organization of society is illustrated in the very opening of the Declaration of Independence.

The "Laws of Nature and of Nature's God" refers to reason. The document in effect asserts that by reason alone one can see that the American colonists are equal in their nature to the people of Britain—both alike have unalienable rights, specifically the rights to "Life, Liberty and the pursuit of Happiness." This "self-evident," fundamental equality was the foundation on which Americans declared independence from Great Britain.

In a borrowing from the social-contract theory common to Enlightenment thinking, Jefferson notes that individuals contract with the government to maintain their individual rights. It is the function and duty of government to secure those rights. When it fails to live up to that contract or actually destroys individuals' rights, it has violated the contract, and the people have the right to change the government, through peaceful means or otherwise.

## The Influence of the Declaration on the Constitution

The greater part of the Declaration of Independence, often referred to as the "lawyer's brief," lists the specific complaints against King George III of Great Britain, with concrete examples of how he violated the social contract with the American colonists. While not nearly as well known as the opening sections of the declaration, this lawyer's brief is significant in that it enumerates the most important political rights guaranteed by the U.S. Constitution. For example, the complaint that the king allowed the military to be independent of civilian control is remedied in Article II of the Constitution by making the president, a civilian officer, the commander in chief of the armed forces. The practice of taxation without representation is prohibited in Article I of the Constitution, which requires that all tax measures originate in the House of Representatives, the branch of Congress most often elected and thus most responsive to the people's will. Denial of a jury trial for offenses committed against the government is prohibited in the Sixth and Seventh amendments.

*The opening paragraphs of the Declaration of Independence refer to the principles of natural law advanced by Enlightenment theorists.*

*When in the Course of human events, it becomes necessary for one People to dissolve the Political Bands which have connected them with another, and to assume among the Powers of the Earth, the separate and equal Station to which the Laws of Nature and of Nature's God entitle them, a decent Respect to the Opinions of Mankind requires that they should declare the causes which impel them to the Separation.*

*We hold these Truths to be self-evident, that all Men are created equal, that they are endowed by their Creator with certain unalienable Rights, that among these are Life, Liberty and the pursuit of Happiness. That to secure these Rights, Governments are instituted among Men, deriving their just Powers from the Consent of the Governed.*

The philosophy that the Declaration of Independence embodies reflects thinking on the nature, origin, and purposes of government that was widespread among the American colonists. Thus, the document itself is both a call to hold government responsible to those purposes and the rough outline of a plan for organizing a government that would not trample upon the rights of the governed. That outline, tempered by a decade's experience of war and peace, provided the basis for the U.S. Constitution.

*Alex Aichinger*

▲ *Richard Henry Lee, whose Virginian grandfather of the same name had been a signatory of the Declaration of Independence a hundred years earlier, reads from the original document at an Independence Day celebration in Philadelphia in 1876.*

SEE ALSO
- Adams, John • Coercive Acts
- Constitution of the United States
- Continental Congresses
- Franklin, Benjamin • Hancock, John
- Henry, Patrick • Jefferson, Thomas
- Lafayette, Marquis de
- Mercantilism and Colonial Economies
- Navigation Acts • Paine, Thomas
- Revere, Paul • Revolutionary War
- Stamp Act

# Democracy in America

ONE OF THE MOST influential works of travel and observation ever written, Tocqueville's *Democracy in America* examines how various characteristics of the young American republic in the early middle years of the nineteenth century—notably the country's political freedom, social equality, and political institutions—relate to one another within the context of a democratic society in the process of forming itself. The book has come to be considered an essential document on the workings of American political life.

▼ *A portrait by Théodore Chassériau (1819–1856) of Alexis de Tocqueville, perhaps the most perceptive foreigner ever to have recorded observations of the United States.* Democracy in America *ranks highly among studies of the American experience.*

*Democracy in America* was written by Alexis de Tocqueville, a young French nobleman, who in 1831 traveled throughout the territory of the United States and carefully recorded observations about American political life and institutions and their underlying principles. The first volume of his study was published in 1835, and the second followed in 1840. The work was considered an immense success and highly esteemed in both France and the United States.

### Equality of Condition

The first volume of *Democracy in America* consists of an examination of democracy and

## ALEXIS DE TOCQUEVILLE ■ 1805–1859

Alexis de Tocqueville was born in Verneuil-sur-Seine on July 29, 1805, to an aristocratic French family. At the age of sixteen, he enrolled in the Collège Royal in Metz and studied philosophy. At the age of eighteen, he began studying law in Paris. His views became increasingly liberal, in marked opposition to his father's royalist tendencies. After 1830 Tocqueville's father lost most of his political influence. In 1831 the younger Tocqueville, prompted by his political ideals, decided to travel to and through the United States to study the new country's political system.

In 1835 Tocqueville married Mary Motley, an Englishwoman; the match did not please his family, however. In 1840, with the appearance of the second volume of *Democracy in America,* a significant measure of public recognition came to Tocqueville. In 1849 he was elected to France's national legislative assembly, but he was dismissed shortly afterward and suffered a breakdown.

In his last years Tocqueville's writing focused on French history, particularly on the events leading to the French Revolution. He died of tuberculosis on April 16, 1859.

liberty. One of its principal themes concerns the preservation of liberty in a society that regards equality as an ideal. Tocqueville observed that American society exhibited a high degree of egalitarian interaction and in this respect was different from European societies, where aristocratic norms were the rule.

In America the relative equality of condition had led to democratic tendencies. Tocqueville noted that the inhabitants of America had so far been successful in preserving a balance between equality and liberty through their institutions and laws, which acted as a check to keep democracy from turning into a tyranny of the majority.

The rights of freedom of association, of the press, and of religion are also excellent means of preventing inequality from becoming exaggerated. These basic human freedoms enable participation in the political process and allow the voices of all citizens to be heard.

## Dangers of Democracy

The second volume focuses more on the individual, on how democratic ideas affect society and its values, and on the abuse of freedom. It explores the possibly dangerous consequences of the democratic process: the assignment of a high proportion of power to the legislative branch of government and the excessive drive toward equality, materialism, and individualism.

As it provides the most direct representation of the popular will, the legislative branch tends to gain the most power in a democratic system. Such a powerful body requires institutional checks to prevent it from becoming tyrannical. An excessive drive toward equality is even more dangerous. If all people are truly equal, no individual or group can gain power over others, and the majority rules. Tocqueville warns that majority-rule democratic societies may quickly become despotic and disallow freedom of action and even free-

*With Gustave de Beaumont, Alexis de Tocqueville visited North America in 1831 to study the U.S. penal system (though he was really interested in a much broader study of American society and institutions). By the time their report,* On the Penitentiary System in the United States and Its Application to France, *was published in 1833 (it was mainly Beaumont's work), Tocqueville had become eager to start on what became* Democracy in America. *Beaumont drew this ink-and-watercolor illustration of a penitentiary in Pennsylvania in 1831.*

▶ *In this 1848 lithograph by Augustus Kollner, the House of Representatives meets in the Chamber of Representatives in the Capitol. Tocqueville's* Democracy in America *warned that a democratic form of government was not in itself a guarantee against tyranny.*

dom of thought. This kind of despotism can become worse than the rule of the most brutal tyrant.

### An Enduring Influence

It is a curious fact that the vast majority of American historians and public officials, whatever their political views and however deep their differences, agree that *Democracy in America* is a crucial text for anyone seeking to understand the way American governance took shape. For this reason alone, the book may be justly regarded as a historic achievement.

In the late 1990s the cable television station C-SPAN followed the route of Tocqueville's journey and broadcast live interviews and call-in shows from the places he had visited. The monthlong focus on American political institutions in their historical context prompted a wide-ranging public discussion on the nature and extent of democratization and the growth of egalitarian tendencies during the many decades since Tocqueville's own time. The one aspect of the discussion that might have surprised Tocqueville was the virtual absence of worry that American democratization had gone too far.

*Matus Dobsovic*

*Tocqueville recognized the importance of the role of individual involvement in the political processes of a society. The relative equality of social condition, he noted, is preserved and enhanced by the impact of the people on their government.*

*Therefore, in reality it is the people who rule. Although they have a representative government, it is quite clear that the opinions, biases, concerns and even the passions of the people can encounter no lasting obstacles preventing them from exercising a day-to-day influence upon the conduct of society.*

DEMOCRACY IN AMERICA

### SEE ALSO
- Constitution of the United States
- Declaration of Independence
- Elections • Executive System
- Federalist Papers
- Jacksonian Democracy • Judicial System
- Press • Suffrage

# Democratic Party

THE DEMOCRATIC PARTY was created after the presidential election of 1824 to defeat John Quincy Adams and bring Andrew Jackson to the presidency. The goal of its creators was to drive the slavery issue out of federal politics by revivifying the economic issues formerly contested by the Federalists and the Jeffersonian Republicans. From their beginnings Democrats associated themselves with the memory of the defunct Democratic-Republican Party of Thomas Jefferson.

## The First Party System

All three branches of the U.S. government in the first administration of George Washington were dominated by federalists—that is to say, those who came to office in the expectation of cooperating in the implementation of the new Constitution. Within a very short time, however, they began to disagree among themselves. While the secretary of the treasury, Alexander Hamilton, wanted the federal government to assume the debts of the states as its own debts, to subsidize industry, and to manage the government debt through a congressionally chartered bank, some opposed Hamilton on these questions; these men styled themselves Republicans. They also opposed the direction of Washington's foreign policy, which, despite the French treaties of 1778, steered a neutral course in the Napoleonic Wars. Republicans would have sided with the new French republic against the European monarchies, including Britain.

By 1793 congressional opponents of Washington and Hamilton had formed a tangible party—a group whose voting behavior is cohesive across a range of issues. The Republicans lost successive fed-

◀ *Thomas Jefferson served as the third president of the United States from 1801 until 1809. When the Democratic Party was formed in the 1820s, it identified itself with Jefferson's Democratic-Republican Party and adopted similar views on economic and constitutional questions. This oil portrait of Jefferson was painted in 1800 by Rembrandt Peale.*

eral elections, but they succeeded in mobilizing popular opinion through newspapers and public festivals throughout the United States. Federalists, who were less enamored of the idea of truly popular government, proved slow to emulate the Republicans' success at party organization.

## Growing Antagonism

In 1798, in the midst of the so-called Quasi War with France, President John Adams signed into law a series of measures intended to secure the country against subversion by pro-French elements.

These Alien and Sedition Acts struck the Republicans (now sometimes called Democratic-Republicans) as threatening the constitutional order.

Thomas Jefferson and James Madison responded by drafting the Virginia and Kentucky Resolutions of 1798. With the resolutions those two state legislatures staked out the Republican understanding of the Constitution: the states formed the fed-

eral government, which therefore was ultimately responsible to the states. In case of unconstitutional and dangerous behavior by the federal government, the states (in Virginia's language) "are in duty bound to interpose" to prevent implementation of the threatening policy within their respective territories.

▼ *This satirical cartoon by H. Clay Quitting depicts the major candidates in the presidential election of 1824; from left to right, John Quincy Adams, William H. Crawford, and Andrew Jackson.*

These measures elicited negative commentary from ten states north of Virginia. In the end, however, Jefferson's prediction that Americans would weary of the taxes associated with the Federalists' Quasi War military buildup proved accurate: he and his party won the election of 1800, and the offending acts were allowed to expire.

## Republican Dominance and Decline

The first two decades of the nineteenth century were dominated so thoroughly by the Republican Party that the Federalist Party ceased to exist. When James Monroe, the third consecutive two-term Virginia Republican president, was reelected in 1820, he received all but one electoral vote.

Monroe's approach to statecraft was nonsectional and nonpartisan. Not only did he sign the Missouri Compromise into law in 1820 despite overwhelming opposition from his home region, but he allowed the Republican Party to atrophy virtually to the point of nonexistence. Thus, in 1824 the former Federalist John Quincy Adams secured election as president in the House of Representatives. Adams had come second in the electoral college (to Andrew Jackson), but the influence of Henry Clay, the Speaker, swung the House vote to him. When Clay was appointed secretary of state almost immediately, the Jackson camp condemned what they perceived to be a "corrupt bargain." John C. Calhoun, the vice president, was persuaded that the federal government was now controlled by selfish sectional interests unconcerned with the common good—as he understood it.

## Democratic Unity and Division

Calhoun's solution was to advise Senator Martin Van Buren of New York to write to

▲ *Martin Van Buren, who became vice president in 1832 and was elected president in 1836, was an early architect of the Democratic Party. This undated portrait depicts him as a young man, well before his rise to the presidency.*

Thomas Ritchie, the editor of the *Richmond Enquirer*, with a proposition: a coalition of "the plain republicans of the north and the planters of the south." Thus was born the Democratic Party. Its goal was to put aside issues concerning slavery, such as those at stake in the Missouri Crisis (1819–1820), and return the federal government to the states' rights posture of Jefferson and Madison.

Jackson was handily elected president in 1828, and proved devoted to states' rights. Jackson's key federal initiative was removal of American Indians from the territory east of the Mississippi River. For the moment, the Democratic Party was the only party.

In dissent, however, stood Calhoun. He had broken with the Democratic Party during the Nullification Crisis (1832–1833), when President Jackson threatened to invade South Carolina unless that state repealed the ordinance nullifying the federal tariff. Fifteen years later Calhoun counseled peace between North and South: if it had been difficult to resolve the Missouri issue in 1820, think how hard it would be to agree on the future of slavery in the extensive lands just conquered from Mexico.

### The Civil War

Calhoun died in 1850, and his forecast proved correct: the North and the South could not agree over slavery in the territories gained from the Mexican War. In 1860 the states that voted Democratic in the presidential election (the southern states) seceded from the Union. A Lincoln administration, they said, would impose tax policies contrary to southern interests and threatened the future of slavery.

While they were a small, discredited minority in the Union, Democrats dominated the Confederacy in the South. Union Democrats' insistence that many of

Abraham Lincoln's policies were unconstitutional fell on deaf ears. Ironically, just as the Union won the war, a southern Democrat, Andrew Johnson of Tennessee, succeeded to the presidency.

▲ In 1876 the Democratic candidate Samuel Tilden won the popular vote but lost the presidential election by one electoral vote to Rutherford B. Hayes.

## INTERPRETING THE CONSTITUTION

For the first sessions of Congress to legislate as Alexander Hamilton asked them to do, they had to accept his approach to constitutional interpretation. Hamilton held—as he said in a private memorandum to President Washington—that the Congress could legislate in any way that the Constitution did not prohibit. Secretary of State Thomas Jefferson, for his part, insisted that Congress could legislate only concerning matters specifically enumerated in the Constitution. This disagreement became a major point of distinction between the parties and remained one for the next 125 years.

## CHRONOLOGY

**1792**
The new Democratic-Republican and Federalist parties contest federal and state elections.

**1820**
James Monroe is reelected president; the Federalist Party ceases to exist, and the Democratic-Republican Party begins to atrophy.

**1824**
The election of John Quincy Adams spurs John C. Calhoun, Martin Van Buren, and Andrew Jackson to form the Democratic Party.

**1833**
Sectional issues—states' rights, tariffs, slavery—begin to divide the Democratic Party.

**1860**
North-South Democratic division ensures the election of Abraham Lincoln as president.

**1876**
A partisan commission awards the disputed presidential election to the Republican candidate, Rutherford B. Hayes, who promptly ends Reconstruction.

**1877**
Democrats recapture southern state governments, which will remain in their hands for a century. They become the party of limited government and noninterference in foreign affairs until Woodrow Wilson's presidency thirty-five years later.

## Reconstruction and Beyond

When the war ended, the Republican Party moved to remake the South radically. Johnson, faithful to the Jacksonian position of states' rights without secession, opposed Republicans every step of the way. His veto of the Civil Rights Bill of 1866 prompted Congress to propose the Fourteenth Amendment—a process that did not require presidential cooperation. Democrats in southern states, meanwhile, generally opposed surrender of their states' primary place in the Union, and so Republicans insisted that they ratify the amendment before they could come back into the Union.

The Democratic Party remained the majority party among white Americans after the war, as it had been before, a fact that helps to explain Republican hesitance to let the South back into Congress and the Union (the Democratic Party would be the "white man's party" in the South for a century). With the Fifteenth Amendment (1870), Republicans hoped to add black southerners to Republican strength in the South. Nonetheless, by the time Reconstruction ended in 1877, Democrats had recaptured southern state governments, and the Republican Party was clearly understood to be the party of most of the North.

The Compromise of 1876, by which Reconstruction was ended, left blacks in the South effectively in the hands of their old masters, who would no longer have to deal with military occupation, in exchange for the abandonment of the just claim of the Democratic candidate, Governor Samuel Tilden of New York, to the presidency. States' rights and associated Jeffersonian maxims remained part of the Democratic creed until 1933.

*Kevin R. C. Gutzman*

SEE ALSO
• Adams, John • Adams, John Quincy
• Alien and Sedition Acts
• Calhoun, John C.
• Civil War • Hamilton, Alexander
• Jackson, Andrew • Jefferson, Thomas
• Johnson, Andrew • Lincoln, Abraham
• Monroe, James • Nullification
• Republican Party • Slavery
• Van Buren, Martin
• Virginia and Kentucky Resolutions
• Washington, George

# Dix, Dorothea

DOROTHEA DIX (1802–1887) was a campaigner for better health care and services for the mentally ill and blind in the nineteenth century. By 1880 her political activities had resulted in the construction of numerous mental hospitals, with Dix playing a direct role in founding thirty-two of them. She was also an ardent crusader for prison reform.

*A photograph from 1840 of Dorothea Dix, a tireless worker for better care for the mentally ill and later the superintendent of U.S. Army nurses during the Civil War.*

Dorothea Lynde Dix was born in Hampden, Maine, on April 4, 1802, the eldest child of Mary and Joseph Dix. At that time Maine was a frontier area and still part of Massachusetts, and life was not easy for the family. Joseph Dix was an itinerant preacher who also sold religious tracts, which the young Dorothea spent hours stitching. Mary Dix was often unable to cope with the difficulties of raising three children in the impoverished conditions in which the family lived.

To escape this unhappy childhood, Dorothea left home at age twelve and went to live with her grandmother and later an aunt in Boston. An avid reader, Dix was teaching primary school children in Worchester, Massachusetts, by age fourteen. She later opened a more formal school in Boston when she was nineteen. Dix, who was a devout Christian, also had successfully published religious tracts and elementary textbooks by age twenty-two. One of her books, *Conversations on Common Things*, went through sixty editions.

Dix was often in poor health because of trouble with her lungs. In 1836 Dix was traveling in Europe to recuperate when she became ill in England and was unable to continue on to Rome. While resting in England, she met Elizabeth Frye, a prison reformer; Samuel Tuke, the administrator of the York Retreat for the Mentally Disordered; and others active in humanitarian causes, including treatment of the the mentally ill. Dix soon embraced their beliefs.

## A Champion of the Mentally Ill

When Dix returned to the United States, she settled in the Boston area. Her grandmother had died and left her financially sound. As part of her humanitarian work, she visited the East Cambridge prison women's ward on March 28, 1841, to teach Sunday school classes. While there, Dix was shocked at its conditions and appalled that mentally ill women were confined in dirty, dark cells with hardened criminals. At this time people who suffered from mental illness were usually either in prison, at home, or in poorhouses. Few institutions existed to provide good care to the mentally ill. Seeing the prisoners chained to the walls, sparsely clothed, underfed, filthy,

and with no source of heat, Dix vowed to work to ensure the mentally ill humane treatment.

She embarked upon a politically ambitious plan. First, she surveyed Massachusetts jails and poorhouses that housed the mentally ill. She then meticulously documented their substandard living conditions. With detailed information regarding the horrific living situations forced upon the mentally ill, she composed a report. Because women were not allowed to participate in politics at this time, Dix could not present her account to the Massachusetts legislature. Therefore, Samuel Gridley Howe, a friend and fellow reformer, submitted the report for her.

In 1843 Howe delivered Dix's "Memorial to the Massachusetts Legislature." Her findings created an uproar among officials; a few even claimed she exaggerated conditions at the state's facilities.

Some legislators pointed out that Massachusetts did not have the money to renovate its hospitals. Nevertheless, Dix persuaded some influential men to help in her campaign, and together they succeeded

---

*Dorothea Dix wrote many reports in which she detailed the harsh treatment afforded the mentally ill and the appalling conditions existing in jails, workhouses, and poorhouses. The one cited here is perhaps the most famous.*

*I come to present the strong claims of suffering humanity. I come to place before the Legislature of Massachusetts the condition of the miserable, the desolate, the outcast. I come as the advocate of helpless, forgotten, insane, and idiotic men and women, of beings sunk to a condition from which the most unconcerned would start with real horror, of beings wretched in our prisons, and more wretched in our almshouses . . . I proceed, gentlemen, briefly to call your attention to the present state of insane persons confined within this Commonwealth, in cages, closets, cellars, stalls, pens! Chained, naked, beaten with rods, and lashed into obedience.*

"MEMORIAL TO THE MASSACHUSETTS LEGISLATURE" (1843)

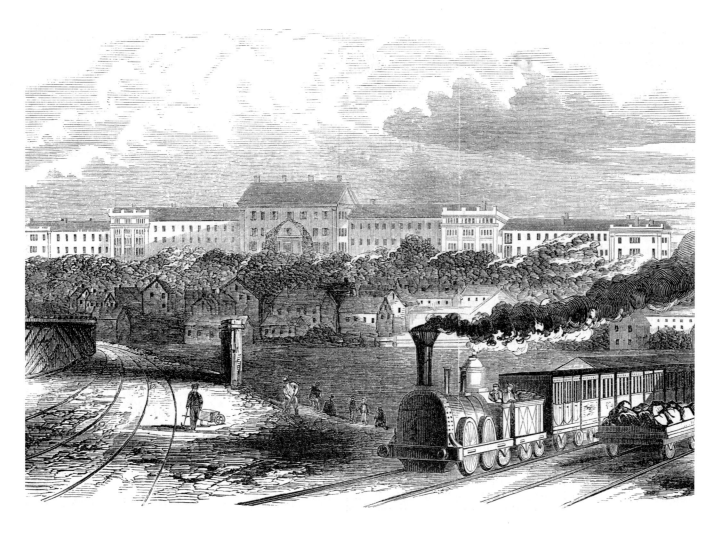

*The massive Worcester Sanatorium in Massachusetts, pictured in the background of this 1852 engraving, dominates the horizon. Dorothea Dix devoted her career to improving the care given to the mentally ill in such facilities.*

in improving and expanding the services offered at the state hospital at Worcester. Henceforward it would provide more humane methods of treatment for the mentally ill, methods that incorporated less use of mechanical restraints and more reliance upon structured activities.

After her Massachusetts victory Dix embarked on a national crusade to lobby for improvements in the other states. Over the next three years she traveled more than 30,000 miles, visiting and writing "memorials" for various state legislatures. Dix journeyed south and was responsible for the reform of nine mental hospitals there. She lobbied tirelessly for better treatment and living conditions for the mentally ill until the Civil War (1861–1865).

## Civil War Service

In the first year of the Civil War, the secretary of war, Simon Cameron, appointed Dix superintendent of nurses for the U.S. Army. even though women were usually not accepted on the battlefield. Approximately two thousand women volunteered to serve as nurses under Dix. She was a strict disciplinarian and at first required that the women be at least thirty years old, "plain looking," and wearing no ornaments of any type on their brown or black uniform. As the war dragged on, the rules came to be ignored as casualities continued to mount and ever more nurses were needed. However, Dix still maintained tight discipline (she was often called Dragon Dix).

By 1863 responsibility for supervision of nurses had been transferred to each hospital and to the U.S. surgeon general, and so Dix was relieved of most of her duties. Yet she continued as a nurse until the war's end and even came to the aid of Union soldiers who were having trouble adjusting to civilian life.

### Retirement Years

Dix spent the rest of her postwar life working for the benefit of the mentally ill. In 1881, too feeble to continue, she retired to the New Jersey State Hospital, a facility she had campaigned to improve earlier in her career. Her activity ceased only with her death on July 18, 1887. Dix is buried in Mount Auburn Cemetery in Cambridge, Massachusetts. In 1983 the U.S. Postal Service featured her image on a postage stamp.

*Deanne Stephens Nuwer*

▲ *The building on the right of this 1862 photograph was used as a Union hospital under the supervision of Dorothea Dix during the Civil War. Some eighty years earlier, the structure had served as the British general Charles Cornwallis's headquarters in the Battle of Yorktown, fought during the last stage of the Revolutionary War.*

SEE ALSO
• Civil War • Great Awakenings
• Law Enforcement and Criminal Justice
• Medicine, Disease, and Epidemics
• Mott, Lucretia • Pierce, Franklin
• Religion and Religious Movements
• Southern Colonies
• Stanton, Elizabeth Cady • Suffrage
• Women's Rights

# Douglas, Stephen A.

BEST KNOWN FOR HIS DEBATES with Abraham Lincoln, Stephen A. Douglas (1813–1861) was one of the most important American politicians of the 1850s. Although he was an ardent supporter of the Union, Douglas is often wrongly identified with the secession of the South, which he consistently opposed.

Stephen A. Douglas was born on April 23, 1813, in Brandon, Vermont, the only son (and second child) of Stephen Arnold Douglass, a physician, and Sarah Fisk Douglass. (Douglas dropped the second s from his last name when he moved to Illinois at the age of twenty.) Stephen's father died when the boy was only two months old. When his mother remarried in 1830, the family moved to upstate New York. From an early age Douglas exhibited a passion for politics (he was a lifelong Democrat), and by the time he had reached twenty, he was already studying to enter the law, a profession that was often a gateway to a political career.

### Go West, Young Man

Douglas rarely acknowledged that he was descended from distinguished old Puritan stock; he preferred to be judged on his personal achievements. That desire, in June 1833, led him to make his way out west. After journeying through Ohio and as far west as Saint Louis, he finally settled in Jacksonville, Illinois, in late 1833; there, he returned to the practice of law. An avid supporter of Andrew Jackson, he first attracted political attention by vigorously defending Jackson's policies at a mass rally. So impressed were his listeners that they picked Douglas up and carried him around the town square on their shoulders. His performance, coupled with his small stature

▲ *U.S. Senate candidate Abraham Lincoln (at the lectern) appears in a celebrated public debate in Illinois with Stephen A. Douglas, his opponent (and the eventual winner of the election), in this 1858 lithograph.*

*In summer 1858 Douglas's compromise on the question of slavery was a source of contention in the Lincoln-Douglas debates. In the second debate, held in Freeport, Douglas responded as follows to Lincoln's question, "Can the people of a Territory in any lawful way . . . exclude slavery from their limits prior to the formation of a State constitution?"*

*I answer emphatically . . . that in my opinion the people of a Territory can, by lawful means, exclude slavery from their limits prior to the formation of a State constitution. . . . It matters not what way the Supreme Court may hereafter decide as to the abstract question whether slavery may or may not go into a Territory under the Constitution, the people have the lawful means to introduce it or exclude it as they please, for the reason that slavery cannot exist a day or an hour anywhere, unless it is supported by local police regulations. Those police regulations can only be established by the local legislature; and if the people are opposed to slavery, they will elect representatives to that body who will by unfriendly legislation effectually prevent the introduction of it into their midst. . . .*

*Whenever the great principle of self-government—the right of the people to make their own Constitution, and come into the Union with slavery or without it, as they see proper—shall again arise, you will find me standing firm in defense of that principle, and fighting whoever fights it.*

▲ *A photograph, taken after 1855, of Stephen A. Douglas, who played a central role in the Compromise of 1850 and ran unsuccessfully for the presidency in 1860. As the country found itself engulfed in war, Douglas, who had opposed Southern secession and vigorously defended the Union, died a broken man in June 1861.*

(he was probably around five feet tall), earned him the lifelong nickname "the Little Giant."

Douglas's political success brought him more legal business than he could handle, and the business, in turn, helped further his political career. Over the next eight years, he held a variety of state offices, including state legislator, secretary of state, and in 1841, justice of the Illinois Supreme Court.

## Mr. Douglas Goes to Washington

Douglas was elected in 1843 to the U.S. House of Representatives, where he quickly cemented his reputation as a defender of Andrew Jackson and as one of the chief proponents of American national expansion. He advocated compromise on the question of slavery, fearing that the issue could destroy the Union. Debating the status of new territory acquired during the Mexican War (1846–1848), Douglas supported the continuation of the Missouri Compromise while arguing that a territory where slaveholding was permitted should be allowed, when it applied for admission to the Union, to adopt a constitution declaring itself a free state—a working principle that came to be called popular sovereignty. Popular sovereignty was codified in the Kansas-Nebraska Act (1854), which Douglas wrote.

## The Lincoln-Douglas Debates and the Presidential Election of 1860

In March 1847 Douglas married Martha Martin. Before her death in 1853, Martha bore Douglas two sons and saw him take his seat as the U.S. senator from Illinois, a position to which he was elected by the Illinois legislature in 1846. He was reelected twice, most famously in 1858, in which year he ran against Abraham Lincoln, with whom he held a series of debates throughout Illinois (although Lincoln lost the senatorial election, the recognition and publicity he garnered helped propel him to the presidency in 1860).

Douglas was an influential figure in Washington. Besides the Kansas-Nebraska Act, the passage of the Compromise of 1850 was also largely his doing, even though it is usually credited to Henry Clay.

Douglas remarried in 1856. His new wife was another southerner, Adele Cutts, the grandniece of James and Dolley Madison; she gave him strength for his final political battle, the presidential election of 1860. Once again, Douglas faced Abraham Lincoln, but this time the Democratic Party was split, with Douglas representing the northern Democrats and Vice President John C. Breckenridge heading the southern Democrats. In the four-way race (the fourth

▲ *Adele Cutts, who became the second wife of the widowed Stephen Douglas in 1856.*

### DID DOUGLAS OWN SLAVES?

Douglas never took a position on the morality of slavery but always treated the question as a political one. When Martha Martin's father, a North Carolina planter, offered the couple a wedding gift of a 2,500-acre Mississippi plantation, including over a hundred slaves, Douglas protested that he had no experience managing such an enterprise and asked his father-in-law to retain ownership of the estate (and all the slaves on it) until his death. When Martin died a year later, he left the plantation not to Douglas but to his daughter alone, and when Martha died in 1853, the property, including the slaves, passed directly to Douglas's sons. While Douglas managed the property for his sons (he even sold it, used the proceeds to purchase another plantation in their name, and moved the slaves to the new location), it is correct to say that he never actually owned a slave.

▲ *This 1860 cartoon depicts Abraham Lincoln "winning the ball" against his opponents Stephen Douglas, John Bell, and John Breckenridge in that year's presidential election.*

man was John Bell, the candidate of the Constitutional Union Party), Lincoln received a plurality (40 percent) of the popular vote but an overwhelming majority (59 percent) of the vote in the electoral college. While Douglas came in second in the popular vote with 29 percent, he received only twelve electoral votes (4 percent).

In early 1861, as the indications that several southern states would soon secede grew unmistakably clear, Douglas, ever the Unionist, spoke out strongly against secession and urged the South to accept the election of Lincoln. Exhausted from the rigors of the presidential-election campaign and a pro-Union, antisecession lecture tour following it, Douglas succumbed to typhoid fever on June 3, 1861. He is buried in Chicago, his home from 1847 on and the site of his death.

*Scott P. Richert*

**SEE ALSO**

- Abolitionism • Civil War
- Compromise of 1850
- Democratic Party
- Expansion and Manifest Destiny
- Jackson, Andrew
- Jacksonian Democracy
- Kansas-Nebraska Act
- Lincoln, Abraham • Madison, Dolley
- Madison, James
- Medicine, Disease, and Epidemics
- Mexican War • Missouri Compromise
- Popular Sovereignty • Secession
- Slavery • State Constitutions
- Third Parties and Alternative Political Movements

# Douglass, Frederick

FREDERICK DOUGLASS (1817–1895) was one of the most outspoken abolitionists of the nineteenth century. An orator and editor, he famously broke with fellow abolitionists over John Brown's raid on Harpers Ferry and on interpretations of the U.S. Constitution.

▲ *This photograph of Frederick Douglass (later hand-colored) was taken by Mathew Brady (1823–1896). Douglass was one of the most prominent abolitionists of his day and a sought-after speaker in Europe and the United States.*

Frederick Douglass was born into slavery in Talbot County, on the Eastern Shore of Maryland, in February 1817. His birth name was Frederick Augustus Bailey; the surname Douglass, like the birth date February 14, was chosen by Douglass himself later in life.

Douglass's mother, Harriet Bailey, was a slave whose ancestors had probably been transported to the West Indies before being brought to Maryland. Douglass was brought up to believe that his father was white; his skin tone was considerably lighter than that of his mother and his grandparents. He had been told that his master, Captain Aaron Anthony, was his father, but in his first autobiography, Douglass declared the matter of "little consequence."

## Early Life

Virtually everything known about Douglass's life before he became a fugitive slave at the age of twenty comes from his three autobiographies. According to Douglass he was raised to the age of six by his grandmother, Betsy, a slave who was married to a free black man, Isaac Bailey. The Baileys had their own cabin in the woods, where Isaac worked as a sawyer and where Betsy enjoyed a certain autonomy from her master's rule.

Douglass claims to have seen his mother only four or five times before she died (when he was around seven years old); he offers no memories of her before he reached age six. Douglass believed it to be a common practice among slaveholders on the Eastern Shore to separate slave children from their mother at an early age, but slaves generally had freedom to visit relatives who lived nearby. The visits that he recounts all occurred after Douglass came

▲ *Frederick Douglass purchased this home, which he named Cedar Hill, in the nation's capital in 1877. It has since become the location of the Frederick Douglass National Historic Site.*

to live with his master at Wye House, the plantation that Captain Anthony managed for Colonel Edward Lloyd, about twelve miles from Douglass's grandparents' cabin. Harriet may have been employed in Lloyd's fields or hired out to a neighbor.

## Escape from Slavery

When Douglass was fifteen, Thomas Auld, the son-in-law of his master, Captain Anthony, hired Douglass out to a local farmer, Edward Covey, who had a reputation for breaking the will of slaves. For six months Douglass endured frequent beatings before deciding to fight back. By wrestling Covey to a standstill, Douglass brought the beatings to an end.

## MISTREATMENT AND KINDNESS FROM SURPRISING SOURCES

A s a child at Wye House, Douglass suffered mistreatment, at the hands not of his master, Captain Anthony, but of Aunt Katy, who ran the household. Herself a slave, Aunt Katy ruled with an iron hand; she whipped Douglass and deprived him of food when she thought him out of line. Both the mistreatment he received and his obvious intelligence brought him to the attention of Captain Anthony's daughter, Lucretia Auld. When Douglass was eight years old, Lucretia and her husband, Captain Thomas Auld, arranged for him to be sent to live with Thomas's brother Hugh in Baltimore. Over Hugh's objection, his wife, Sophia, taught Douglass to read and introduced him to Christianity. Though Douglass would later become convinced that religion was used to justify slavery, he was very devout in his teen years. In fact, when he returned to live with his master, he tried to convert Thomas Auld, believing that conversion would lead Auld to emancipate him.

Douglass then resolved to escape from slavery, but Auld, who had befriended Douglass, thought that escape would be disastrous for the young man. Fearing that Douglass would be captured and sold back into slavery, Auld sent Douglass back to his brother Hugh with the promise that, if Douglass trained as a skilled tradesman, he would be granted his freedom at the age of twenty-five.

Douglass refused to wait. At the age of twenty, in the hope of purchasing freeman's papers, he persuaded Hugh to allow him to hire himself out and to keep his wages. In September 1838, posing as a free seaman, Douglass escaped. He eventually arrived in New York. There he sent for Anna Murray, a free black woman with whom he had been romantically involved in Baltimore, and the two were married. They moved to New Bedford, Massachusetts, and, over forty-four years of marriage, had five children.

## Life as a Freeman

Douglass became active in the abolitionist movement, for which cause he delivered speeches about his experience as a slave. He came to collaborate with William Lloyd Garrison, the publisher of the *Liberator,* the leading abolitionist newspaper. The two men quarreled in the early 1850s, however, when Douglass became convinced that the U.S. Constitution was actually antislavery in intent. (Garrison believed that the Constitution intended to protect slavery, and he often burned copies of the document during his speeches.)

In 1845 Douglass wrote the first of his autobiographies, *Narrative of the Life of Frederick Douglass, an American Slave.* Two years later, he founded the *North Star,* an abolitionist newspaper, which in 1851 became *Frederick Douglass' Paper.* As a publisher, he took on other social issues, including women's suffrage. His second autobiography, *My Bondage and My Freedom,* appeared in 1855.

▼ *This poster advertises "The Fugitive's Song," which Jesse Hutchinson Jr. composed in honor of Frederick Douglass in 1845.*

302

## Abolition and Reconstruction

With Abraham Lincoln's Emancipation Proclamation (1863), Douglass's hopes for the abolition of slavery were realized. After the war he argued that black suffrage did not require an amendment to the Constitution because he regarded citizenship as a national matter, not a state one. (Until the Fourteenth Amendment passed in 1868, Americans were treated as citizens first of their respective states and, second, through their states, as citizens of the United States.)

During Reconstruction, Douglass served in a number of federal posts and eventually moved to Anacostia, in the District of Columbia. His third autobiography, *Life and Times of Frederick Douglass*, was published in 1881, and after the death of his wife, Anna, he remarried in 1884. Helen Pitts, his new wife, was a white woman twenty years his junior who believed strongly in equal rights for women.

**In 1848 Douglass published an open letter, "To My Old Master, Thomas Auld." In it, Douglass declared his lack of malice toward Auld and expressed his desire to return to Maryland as a freeman.**

*You may perhaps want to know how I like my present condition. I am free to say, I greatly prefer it to that which I occupied in Maryland. I am, however, by no means prejudiced against the state as such. . . . It is not that I love Maryland less, but freedom more. You will be surprised to learn that people at the north labor under the strange delusion that if the slaves were emancipated at the south, they would flock to the north. . . . We want to live in the land of our birth, and to lay our bones by the side of our fathers; and nothing short of an intense love of personal freedom keeps us from the south. For the sake of this, most of us would live on a crust of bread and a cup of cold water.*

FREDERICK DOUGLASS,
*MY BONDAGE AND MY FREEDOM*

▶ *The frontispiece and title page to* My Bondage and My Freedom. *In effect a second autobiography, the book was published in 1855.*

*While Douglass was a friend of John Brown, he disagreed strongly with Brown's attempt to advance the cause of abolitionism through violence.*

*The taking of Harper's Ferry, of which Captain Brown had merely hinted before, was now declared as his settled purpose, and he wanted to know what I thought of it. I at once opposed the measure with all the arguments at my command. . . . It would be an attack upon the Federal government, and would array the whole country against us.*

*Captain Brown . . . did not at all object to rousing the nation; it seemed to him that something startling was just what the nation needed. He . . . thought that the capture of Harper's Ferry would serve as notice to the slaves that their friends had come, and as a trumpet to rally them to his standard. . . .*

*He was not to be shaken by anything I could say, but treated my views respectfully, replying that even if surrounded he would find means for cutting his way out; but that would not be forced upon him; he should, at the start, have a number of the best citizens of the neighborhood as his prisoners and that holding them as hostages he should be able, if worse came to worse, to dictate terms of egress from the town.*

*I looked at him with some astonishment, that he could rest upon a reed so weak and broken. . . .*

FREDERICK DOUGLASS, *THE LIFE AND TIMES OF FREDERICK DOUGLASS*

## Death and Burial

On February 20, 1895, Douglass addressed a women's rights convention in Washington, DC. That evening, at his home in Anacostia, while mimicking one of the speakers for the amusement of his wife, he collapsed and died. His body was transported by train to Rochester, New York, where he was buried in Mount Hope Cemetery.

*Scott P. Richert*

**SEE ALSO**

- Abolitionism
- Amendments, Post–Civil War
- Brown, John • Civil War
- Constitution of the United States
- Emancipation Proclamation
- Fugitive Slave Laws
- Garrison, William Lloyd
- Lincoln, Abraham • Race Relations
- Reconstruction • Slavery • Suffrage
- Women's Rights

▼ *Douglass's gravestone. He was buried in Rochester, New York.*

# Dred Scott v. Sandford

**THE JUDGMENT** of the U.S. Supreme Court in the Dred Scott case was one of the events that provoked war between the northern and southern blocs of states, the war that has come to be known as the American Civil War.

## Historical Background

When Thomas Jefferson composed what later became the Northwest Ordinance of 1787, he wrote that "neither slavery nor involuntary servitude" would be allowed in the Northwest Territory. He meant to prohibit bondage of all people, whether they were of black African or white Anglo-Saxon origin.

Earlier still, before the American Revolution, a significant judgment was handed down in a 1772 case that came before the King's Bench in London. A black slave from Jamaica had been brought to London by his master on a business trip. The presiding judge, William Murray, Lord Mansfield (1705–1793), held that, because slavery was not protected by the common law and no statute allowed slavery in England, the slave became free the moment he set foot on English soil. Lord Mansfield's judgment was soon recognized everywhere in the British Empire as the universal law. The fugitive slave clause in the original, unemended Constitution's Article IV, section 2, was understood as a limited exception to the otherwise prevailing rule that a slave who set foot on free soil became free.

Lord Mansfield's rule was adopted by judges in all the American states, both southern and northern. Indeed, thousands of slaves were judicially freed in the South, where, in any event, the strongest American abolition movement was found.

▲ *This portrait of Dred Scott was painted by Louis Schultze (died after 1895). Scott, a slave who claimed freedom on the grounds that he had been taken to parts of the country where slavery was illegal, inadvertently ignited sectional strife when the Supreme Court handed down its controversial ruling in his case.*

In 1838 Chief Justice William Gaston (1778–1844) of the North Carolina Supreme Court even held that, when a slave became free, he became a citizen: "Slaves manumitted here become freemen—and therefore, if born within North Carolina, are citizens of North Carolina—and all free persons born within the State are born citizens of the State."

305

### The Case of Dred Scott

Such was the settled law when in 1846 a slave named Dred Scott brought a suit before the circuit court of Missouri wherein he sought freedom for himself, his wife, and his two daughters. He had been taken by his master, John Sanford, on a tour of military duty into territory declared free by the Missouri Compromise (1820).

*This 1857 edition of* Frank Leslie's Illustrated Newspaper *features a front-page story on the Dred Scott decision that includes illustrations of Dred Scott and his family.*

The law being clear, the circuit judge quickly liberated Scott and his family.

### From Freedom Back to Slavery

A majority of the Missouri Supreme Court, however, reversed the judgment of the circuit court and remanded Scott and his family back to Sanford's custody in defiance of settled law. Justice Hamilton Gamble (1798–1864), writing a learned dissent that reviewed the jurisprudence of Missouri and other southern states, protested, "In this State, it has been recognized from the beginning of the government, as a correct position in law, that a master who takes his slave to reside in a state or territory where slavery is prohibited, thereby emancipates his slave."

Scott then sued his master before the federal circuit court in Saint Louis. By a tangled web of legal maneuvers, the case reached the U.S. Supreme Court, where in 1857 it was decided, in a seven-to-two decision, as *Dred Scott v. Sandford* (the extra *d* is a misspelling that was never corrected in the court documents). Chief Justice Roger B. Taney (1777–1864), speaking for the majority, held that Scott and his family could never become citizens even if emancipated and thus lacked standing to sue in federal courts; so Scott and his family were still slaves. Taney then added that, in any event, the Missouri Compromise was unconstitutional. Two long dissents were written, the better-known one by Justice Benjamin Curtis, who explained why Scott and his family were entitled to their freedom.

In striking down the Missouri Compromise, Chief Justice Taney said, "No word can be found in the Constitution which gives Congress greater power over slave property, or which entitles property of

## BENJAMIN CURTIS ■ 1809–1874

Benjamin Curtis was appointed and confirmed as an associate justice of the U.S. Supreme Court in 1851. His unanswerable dissent in *Dred Scott v. Sandford* is seventy pages of remarkable erudition. He consciously wrote for future generations, lest anybody cast unfair blame on the South and its state courts, which had freed Scott and his family; or on the Founding Fathers of the United States, who had hoped to nudge slavery into extinction as soon as peaceably practicable. After delivering his dissent, Judge Curtis concluded his work on the court and resigned his seat; he then returned to his native Boston, where he undertook a successful law practice.

Curtis was widely respected by moderates in the North and the South. He was deeply saddened by the outbreak of hostilities; in his eyes the war was one of cultural misunderstanding. In 1868 he spoke out in defense of President Andrew Johnson against the factious bill of impeachment voted by the Republican Congress.

▼ *An undated engraving of Roger B. Taney, chief justice of the United States at the time of the Dred Scott decision. His majority opinion, which returned Scott to slavery and declared the Missouri Compromise unconstitutional, convinced some abolitionists that there was no hope for a peaceful end to slavery.*

that kind to less protection than property of any other description." Even at the time, however, it was noted in dissent that William Blackstone (1723–1780), the revered English jurist and legal scholar whose commentaries are still studied closely, had said that "a slave, the moment he lands in England, falls under the protection of the laws, and so far becomes a freeman." The Philadelphia convention that drafted the Constitution also accepted this principle of English law as the law of the American union.

### The Aftermath

The Dred Scott case may be seen as an illustration of the importance of giving everybody, however humble or weak, the benefit of established law. The decision had many ironic consequences, some tragic, some merely droll. Public passions

## A PUBLIC MEETING

### WILL BE HELD ON

### THURSDAY EVENING, 2D INSTANT,

at 7; o'clock, in ISRAEL CHURCH, to consider the atrocious decision of the Supreme Court in the

## DRED SCOTT CASE,

and other outrages to which the colored people are subject under the Constitution of the United States.

## C. L. REMOND,
### ROBERT PURVIS,

and others will be speakers on the occasion. Mrs. MOTT, Mr. M'KIM and B. S. JONES of Ohio, have also accepted invitations to be present.
All persons are invited to attend. Admittance free.

▶ *This poster advertises a meeting in 1857 to discuss the Dred Scott case. The decision was highly unpopular in the North, where some cited it as evidence of a "slave power" conspiracy at work in the federal government.*

*Despite the fact that the main author of the Declaration of Independence, the Virginian Thomas Jefferson, was the father of the southern abolition movement, Chief Justice Roger Taney of the U.S. Supreme Court, in holding that neither a slave nor the descendant of a slave could ever become a citizen, even if granted freedom, claimed that the authors of the Declaration understood*

*. . . the meaning of the language they used and how it would be understood by others; and they knew that it would not in any part of the civilized world be supposed to embrace the Negro race. . . . The unhappy black race were separated from the white by indelible marks, and laws long before established, and were never thought of or spoken of except as property.*

OPINION OF THE MAJORITY, *DRED SCOTT V. SANDFORD*

prompted the secession of eleven southern states from the Union. As it happens, Scott and his family were granted freedom by their master shortly after the judgment was handed down. Soon after, as war ravaged the country, General Robert E. Lee, commander in chief of all Confederate land forces, proposed a plan for granting slaves freedom on a broad scale. Lee, backed up by most of the Confederate army and by widespread popular southern sentiment, was derided by others as an abolitionist.

*John Remington Graham*

SEE ALSO
• Civil War
• Declaration of Independence
• Fugitive Slave Laws • Jefferson, Thomas
• Judicial System • Missouri Compromise
• Race Relations • Slavery

unleashed by the decision inevitably aggravated sectional ill feeling–the people of the South were widely blamed for the judgment of the Supreme Court–which in turn

# Dutch Colonization

**DUTCH ENTREPRENEURS** and settlers, first exploring and then controlling the Hudson River valley from 1609 until 1664, established the territory of New Netherland, a chain of forts, towns, and trading posts along the Hudson River, in what is now New York State. Many of their settlements developed into cities that still exist and flourish. Albany was once the Dutch outpost of Fort Orange, and New York City was originally New Amsterdam.

In 1609, two years after the English established their colony at Jamestown, in Virginia, the Englishman Henry Hudson was hired by the Dutch East India Company to find a northeast passage to India. Hudson sailed north along the coast of Norway as instructed, but his ship, the *Half Moon,* was repeatedly blocked by ice. Rather than return in defeat, Hudson turned west and crossed the Atlantic Ocean to seek instead a northwest passage to the Pacific above the North American continent. Arriving off the coast near what is now Cape Cod, Massachusetts, Hudson sailed south; when he reached the mouth of the Hudson River, he entered it and sailed north until the water was too shallow to continue (at present-day Albany). On his return to Europe, Hudson claimed the entirety of the Hudson River valley for his Dutch employers.

## A Rich Land

Beaver pelts were especially prized in Europe—they had medicinal uses besides being sought for warmth—and Hudson's enthusiastic report of fur-trade prospects along the Hudson River enticed Dutch enterpreneurs. Expeditions produced maps of the Hudson River region, and in 1614 it was officially named New Netherland. The mapped region included parts of present-day New York, Connecticut, Delaware, and New Jersey—the area of the Northeast's largest rivers. With these rivers providing easy access to beavers and other animals as well as to the Atlantic, early adventurers and fur traders formed business alliances with the native peoples, alliances that facilitated further exploration and settlement.

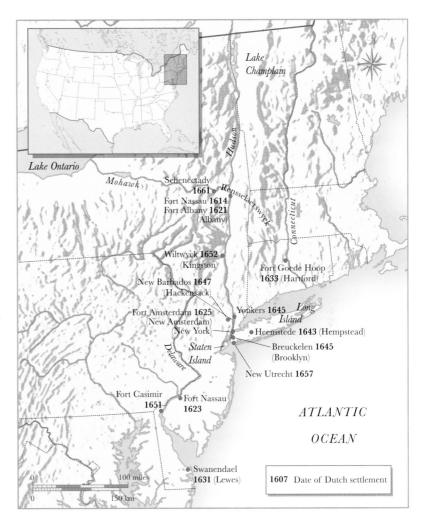

*The territory of New Netherland was centered on the Hudson River valley and extended from the mouth of the Delaware River in the south to the mouth of the Connecticut River in the north.*

## The Dutch West India Company

Like the English colonists in Virginia, many Dutch settlers preferred the more profitable fur trade to farming. The Dutch West India Company was formed by Dutch merchants in 1621 and soon came to monopolize trade in the region. Impressed by the company's success, the Dutch parliament gave the organization an exclusive

*This illustration, copied from a nineteenth-century painting, depicts American Indians trading furs on board Henry Hudson's ship.*

charter to oversee all Dutch projects in the Western Hemisphere. The company was restricted from formal military action, such as the declaration of war, but otherwise it had nearly complete administrative and judicial power over the territory of New Netherland.

To defend river access to the West India Company's trade in the Hudson Valley, Fort Amsterdam (later New Amsterdam) was built on the southern tip of Manhattan Island. Fort Orange and other inland forts were established as fur-trading outposts. Because New Netherland was an economic enterprise, the company was reluctant to establish family-oriented settlements. Within three years, however, thirty families sponsored by the company arrived to colonize the territory, operate trading posts, and grow food for the company's increasing number of employees.

## Transporting Dutch Culture and Law

In 1624 the Dutch parliament decided to reconstitute New Netherland as an overseas province of the Dutch republic and open it up for settlement. The West India Company and other private traders were ordered to vacate most of New Netherland to make way for the settlers. The logical location for the new center of commerce was the mouth of the Hudson River, since it provided access to both the ocean and the main waterway to the northernmost territory, where European goods and wampum were bartered for the American Indians' beaver pelts.

The new Dutch colonists were required to adopt the laws of Holland, which included the provision of religious freedom. The settlers decided to further extend this provision by establishing a right to freedom of

t' Fort nieuw Amsterdam op de Manhatans.

◀ *The Hartgers View (c. 1626–1628), the oldest view of the island of Manhattan, was published in Amsterdam by Joost Hartgers. The caption reads "Fort New Amsterdam on the Manhattan."*

conscience as well as religion. Their aim in so doing was to maximize the attractiveness of their colony to other potential settlers.

## Obstacles to Development

Hampered as New Netherland was by poor administration, colonization proceeded slowly. The West India Company prohibited manufacturing, placed restrictions on commerce, and controlled crop planting—all with dismal results. In addition, European farming practices were found to be unsuitable to the new land, and so settlers were forced to buy food from the natives. The company's policy of patroonship added to the difficulty of attracting new colonists. Each patroon (proprietor of an estate) was granted privileges and a large land lease in exchange for bringing fifty new settlers to the colony. Patroons exercised near-feudal powers over their landholdings—the right to establish civil and criminal courts and to

appoint local officers—and settlers were required to pay their patroon in money, goods, or services.

Both patroons and settlers were governed by a series of directors general appointed by the West India Company's hierarchy. Most notable among them were the third, Peter Minuit, and the seventh and last, Peter Stuyvesant.

### MANHATTAN PURCHASE

In 1626 Peter Minuit was sent to Manhattan with instructions to improve and expand the colonization efforts. Following the Dutch policy that required formal purchase of all land to be assigned to settlers, Minuit bought what is now called Manhattan Island from the Manahatta Indians for sixty guilders ($24) worth of trade goods. The Manahattas had no concept of the sale of land; they thought they were merely granting hunting and fishing rights to the Dutch, who would eventually move on. After his "purchase," Minuit officially established New Amsterdam and strengthened Fort Orange at the northern end of the territory, about 150 miles away.

## CHRONOLOGY

**1609**
Henry Hudson sails to North America and explores the Hudson River valley.

**1614**
New Netherland is mapped and named.

**1621**
The Dutch charter the West India Company to oversee colonization.

**1624**
The first families settle in New Netherland.

**1626**
Peter Minuit purchases Manhattan Island.

**1629**
The West India Company approves the patroon plan for colonization.

**1639**
The West India Company ends its trade monopoly.

**1655**
Stuyvesant conquers New Sweden in the Delaware Valley; the Peach War, between Dutch settlers and American Indians, takes place in October.

**1664**
Stuyvesant surrenders New Amsterdam to the English after a surprise attack.

**1665–1667**
In the Second Anglo-Dutch War, the Dutch regain and then lose New York to the English.

**1672–1674**
In the Third Anglo-Dutch War, New York is recaptured by the Dutch, and New Netherland is restored as a Dutch colony.

**1674**
The Treaty of Westminster returns the Dutch colonies in America to the English.

## American Indians and the Other Colonies

The majority of Dutch forts were established in territory occupied by Algonquian-speaking tribes, the primary traders of pelts. Within a few years, however, the beaver population was depleted in the lower river valleys, and trade was expanded among the inland natives. In the north, Dutch authorities had been maintaining peace between fur traders and the tribe of the Iroquois Confederacy, although fraud and corruption were common. At Fort Orange the Mohawks were allied with the Dutch, who were equipping them to fight against other tribes allied with the French. In the lower Hudson Valley, colonists who had begun to farm viewed the Indians as a hindrance; their battles with the local natives created tension and suspicion between settlers and tribes.

From the 1620s to the 1640s, successive directors general were less than diplomatic in attempts to increase their holdings. Dutch expeditions encroached on lands claimed by English and Swedish settlers and "bought" land from the local Indians. Still, the colony grew slowly until 1639, when the West India Company, finally realizing that the limitations imposed by its trade monopoly lay behind the slow growth, opened New Netherland to non-Dutch investors.

## Strong Leadership Arrives

In 1647, when Peter Stuyvesant became director general, he found a colonial society greatly weakened by years of conflict, sudden growth, and a string of ineffective administrators. As a result of open trade, New Amsterdam's population was growing rapidly and becoming more diversified (only 50 percent were Dutch) To establish control and assert his authority, Stuyvesant issued new edicts and enforced old ones. His attempts to restrict religion went too far for the freedom-conscious colonists, however, and the result was resentment and opposition.

Stuyvesant's reign was characterized by constant clashes with the English, the Swedish, and the native tribes. He conquered New Sweden (in what is now Delaware), New England threatened invasion of New Amsterdam, and Indians attacked the area around Manhattan (notably during late 1655 in what came to be called the Peach War). Yet under his

## PETER STUYVESANT ■ c. 1610–1672

**B**orn the son of a clergyman in the Dutch province of Friesland, Peter Stuyvesant developed an early interest in military life; he served in the West Indies and lost a leg in battle on Saint Martin Island before returning to Holland in 1644. He became known for his dapper dress and silver-banded wooden leg. Although he often had an abrupt, cold manner, he could be sympathetic and affectionate with those he cared for. His wife, Judith, was born in Holland and died in New York fifteen years after Peter. They had one son, Nicholas (1648–1698), and numerous grandchildren and great-grandchildren.

In 1647 Stuyvesant was warmly welcomed by the Dutch colonists in North America when he arrived as director general. Although he attempted to improve the colonists' standard of living, he antagonized the Dutch patroons by challenging their authority over the land; he also had trouble with neighboring colonies for the same reason. Stuyvesant, a staunch adherent of the Dutch Reformed Church, was unsympathetic to any type of religious freedom. A headstrong leader who believed his authority came from God, Stuyvesant ignored the wishes of his constituents, who mostly favored religious tolerance, and even disobeyed orders from Holland. After the surrender of the Dutch colonies to England, he spent his remaining days on his sixty-two-acre farm, the Great Bouwerie, outside the city walls.

▶ *The headstrong Peter Stuyvesant, pictured in an eighteenth-century portrait, governed New Amsterdam with an iron hand until forced to relinquish the colony to the English. The Dutch prospered under his administration.*

> *Peter Stuyvesant ruled with an iron hand and was not slow to threaten severe punishment for any perceived mutiny from the colonists.*
>
> *If any one, during my administration, shall appeal, I will make him a foot shorter, and send the pieces to Holland and let him appeal in that way.*
>
> QUOTED IN JOHN ROMEYN BRODHEAD,
> *HISTORY OF THE STATE OF NEW YORK*

▶ *This oil, painted in 1932 by Jean Leon Gerome Ferris as part of a series called* The Pageant of a Nation, *shows Peter Stuyvesant standing on the shore in 1664; residents of New Amsterdam plead with him not to open fire on the British warships, which have gathered in the harbor in readiness to claim the territory for Britain.*

stern guidance New Netherland prospered. As problems with Indians decreased and temporary profit seekers were replaced with stable families, the colony began to produce a huge influx of wealth for the Dutch homeland. Other nations soon envied the profits spilling out of the Hudson River valley.

### Anglo-Dutch Wars

For years the English and Dutch had been vying for power over colonies throughout the world; the First Anglo-Dutch War took place between 1652 and 1654. In 1664, during a time of relative peace, an English fleet carried out a surprise attack and, meeting minimal resistance, captured New Amsterdam. Thanks in part to his unpopularity, Stuyvesant was unable to raise a defense and was forced to surrender the colony to the English, who renamed it New York.

Over the next few years the Dutch prepared their navy for the battle to regain the colony. During the Second (1665–1667) and Third (1673–1674) Anglo-Dutch Wars, New Amsterdam was captured and lost more than once, until finally, with the Treaty of Westminster, signed by Holland and England in 1674, hostilities ended and the Dutch withdrew all claims on the colony.

Although with the treaty the direct involvement of the Netherlands in North America was effectively ended, Dutch immigration continued, with major western settlements later developing once access to the Mississippi River was obtained.

*Karen Aichinger*

SEE ALSO
• British Colonization
• Colonial Wars
• Iroquois Confederation • Jamestown
• Mercantilism and Colonial Economies
• Native Americans
• New England Colonies

# Education

EARLY SETTLERS in the American colonies appreciated the importance of education, and besides teaching their own children at home, they took a number of steps to create schools and colleges. It was not until the 1800s, however, that the roots of the modern American educational system were in place.

### Education in New England

Deep, regionally based differences over how to approach the issue of education existed in the earliest British colonies in North America. Jamestown, the first permanent English settlement, was founded in 1607, but initially there was little attention paid to education in Virginia. In New England, on the other hand, education was a primary concern of the first settlers, in whose minds education and religion were closely linked. The Puritans who founded the New England colonies believed people needed to be taught to read so that they could read and understand the Bible. The

New Englanders also saw school as a means to reinforce their religious beliefs by inculcating them in the young.

In the 1630s several New England communities created informal schools that taught grammar, arithmetic, and religion. In addition, in 1636 the Massachusetts colonial council voted to establish Harvard College; the college was founded in order to prepare young men to become ministers of the Gospel. In 1642 the Massachusetts legislature passed the Common Schools Ordinance. This law required towns with a population of more than a hundred to create a grammar school (commonly known

◄ *This 1713 engraving depicts a New England dame school. At a dame school children of the neighborhood were taught the rudiments of reading, writing, and arithmetic by a woman in her own home.*

as a Latin School because instruction was in Latin) to prepare students to attend Harvard College or colleges back in England. Five years later, another law was enacted that required towns with at least fifty people to employ a teacher (although a town did not have to build a school until the population reached one hundred). The 1647 law also allowed towns to tax people to pay for schools and gave communities the right to compel parents to send their children to school. Other New England colonies soon passed similar measures to provide education; Connecticut did so in 1650, for example.

## Education in Virginia

In the Virginia colony a less formal and juridical approach to education was the norm. What early laws there were assumed that the burden of education was to be borne by parents and guardians. For example, legislation enacted in 1642 simply required guardians to provide education to their orphan charges. In 1646 another law gave judges the power to remove children from parents who did not provide basic education; the standards were not defined but were left to the judgment of the court.

The first effort to establish a formal school was made in 1635, when a colonist left two hundred acres in his will to fund the building of a school and the hiring of a teacher. However, it was not until 1647 that the school—a public, free school—was finally founded. Private schools, known as academies, were later established in Virginia to educate the children of prosperous families. In 1730 a second public school was established in Virginia.

Following the lead of Virginia and Massachusetts, Maryland established a

school in 1696, and Pennsylvania did so in 1698. In 1724 the South Carolina legislature passed a measure requiring every county to provide a school for children whose parents could not afford tuition at private academies.

The first college in the South—the second in the nation—was created in 1693, when William and Mary College was chartered in Williamsburg, Virginia. By the start of the American Revolution some eighty years later, there were nine colleges in the new United States.

▼ The statue of Lord Botetourt, a colonial governor of Virginia, stands before the Wren Building at the College of William and Mary in Williamsburg, Virginia. William and Mary was the second college founded in what became the United States.

## Age Differentiation

In both the northern and the southern colonies, schools were established for different age groups. Younger children, aged six to eight, attended basic schools, commonly called dame schools, since they were often taught by widows or young ladies. Older students went on to attend the Latin schools, where the curriculum concentrated on reading and writing. Students typically had few books or other materials. Throughout the colonies the hornbook was the common instrument of instruction. The hornbook was a child's primer; it was typically a wooden board on which was inscribed basic information, including the alphabet and, usually, the Lord's Prayer. In the late 1600s schools in the North began to use an elementary textbook, the eighty-

A — In *Adam's* Fall We Sinned all.

B — Thy Life to Mend This *Book* Attend.

C — The *Cat* doth play And after slay.

D — A *Dog* will bite A Thief at night.

E — An *Eagles* flight Is out of fight.

F — The Idle *Fool* Is whipt at School.

*◄ This page from a 1721 edition of* The New England Primer *contains part of an illustrated alphabet. The primer, first published in 1690, was used as an educational tool into the nineteenth century.*

five-page *New England Primer*. Arithmetic textbooks became available in the 1780s.

## Education in the Revolutionary and Independence Eras

In the mid-1700s an increasing number of American colonists became convinced that higher education needed to include subjects in addition to religion and the classics. In 1743 Benjamin Franklin formed the American Philosophical Society with the goal of spreading modern ideas and concepts throughout the colonies. In 1751 he established the Philadelphia Academy in Philadelphia to offer an educational alternative to the traditional curriculum. Franklin's school offered courses in practical subjects such as geography, law, and surveying. The academy later became the College of Philadelphia and then the University of Pennsylvania.

*Like Harvard, William and Mary College was founded to spread Christianity and to educate ministers, a fact affirmed by the college's 1727 statutes, which declared the purpose of the institution:*

*That the Churches of America, especially Virginia, should be supplied with good Ministers after the Doctrine and Government of the Church of England; and that the College should be a constant Seminary for this Purpose. . . . That the Indians of America should be instructed in the Christian Religion, and that some of the Indian Youth that are well-behaved and well-inclined, being first well prepared in the Divinity School, may be sent out to preach the Gospel to their Countrymen in their own Tongue*

STATUTES OF THE COLLEGE OF
WILLIAM AND MARY (1727)

In 1779, during the Revolutionary War, Thomas Jefferson proposed that Virginia establish a two-track educational system. Jefferson's plan divided students into two groups. One group would be prepared for the law, the ministry, or medicine, while the second group would be schooled in practical, laboring trades, such as ironwork, shipbuilding, and surveying. Although Jefferson's proposal was not approved at the time, its theme would later be implemented with the creation of vocational schools throughout the United States.

After the Revolution, the Continental Congress made an effort to put in place mandatory universal education. Passed in 1785, the Land Ordinance provided for the setting aside of sections of the land being settled in the western territories to build public schools. In 1787 the Northwest Ordinance declared that a portion of land in all new towns was to be utilized to provide schools. These two laws ensured that the new towns that would soon spring up in the West would have schools.

## Growing State Involvement in Education

Meanwhile, in the established areas in the East, the states increasingly asserted control over local schools. For example, in 1798 Connecticut took authority over the schools out of the hands of church groups and transferred it to local school boards. Other states passed laws that required communities to establish free school in all districts and communities. School curricula were also broadened and regularized. Many of the main principles of present-day education in America were put in place during

▶ *Established in New Haven, Connecticut, in 1701, Yale University, pictured here in an engraving of around 1830, is the third oldest university in the United States.*

## CHRONOLOGY

**1617**
Efforts to create a
college in Virginia fail.

**1636**
Harvard College is
founded in Cambridge,
Massachusetts.

**1701**
Yale University is
founded in New Haven,
Connecticut.

**1740**
South Carolina enacts a
law forbidding the
education of slaves.

**1830**
A school for free African
Americans opens in
Baltimore, Maryland.

**1833**
Oberlin College
(Oberlin, Ohio)
becomes the nation's
first coeducational
university.

**1837**
Horace Mann becomes
head of the
Massachusetts State
Board of Education.

**1839**
The nation's first
teachers college is
founded in
Massachusetts.

**1846**
The first American
school is established in
California (Spanish
mission schools had
existed there since the
late eighteenth
century).

**1856**
The first American
kindergarten facility is
started in Wisconsin.

**1862**
Iowa State University is
founded as the first
land grant college.

the early 1800s through the efforts of Horace Mann and other pioneers of educational theory. After the first public high school opened in Boston in 1821, the states began requiring communities to provide high schools in addition to elementary schools. Massachusetts enacted the first compulsory school-attendance law in 1852, but it was not until the 1880s that a significant number of other states adopted similar laws, and it was not until 1918 that all states had compulsory attendance regulations.

▶ *Harvard (1636) was the first college established in the colonies. Although this statue on the campus supposedly depicts John Harvard, the sculptor had no idea what he looked like, and the statue's true likeness is unknown.*

## AMERICA'S FIRST COLLEGE

Harvard University was founded as Harvard College in 1636 (it was formally renamed Harvard University on September 1, 1779). The college, the first one in what is now the United States, was named after John Harvard, a minister who donated his library and some property after his death to help fund the institution. The college's curriculum was modeled on that followed in British universities of the era, although religion was emphasized in accordance with the primary mission of Harvard: to train ministers. In 1650 control of Harvard was turned over to an incorporated board, the Harvard Corporation. This board continues to run Harvard and is in fact the oldest corporation in the United States.

A number of specialized educational institutions were founded in the early 1800s. The first school for the deaf opened in Connecticut in 1817, and the first institution for the blind was founded in Massachusetts in 1829. The nation's first college for women, Mount Holyoke Seminary, was established in 1837. In 1857 the National Teachers' Association was founded. It later became the National Education Association and is now the largest U.S. teachers' union.

### The Civil War and Reconstruction

Before the conclusion of the Civil War effectively ended slavery in the United States, slaves were not allowed an education. In fact, by the 1830s all of the southern states had laws that forbade educating slaves. Within a decade of the conflict's end, the Thirteenth, Fourteenth, and Fifteenth amendments had been ratified and two civil rights acts had been passed to improve the lot of African Americans, not least in education. The federal Freedmen's Bureau created a number of schools to educate former slaves, and between 1862 and 1870 the federal government spent some six million dollars and engaged more than 9,500 teachers, who came mainly from the North. Nonetheless, there remained notable differences between the educational opportunities available to whites and blacks, especially after the Supreme Court overturned the civil rights acts in 1883. In addition, the economic depression of 1873 constrained public spending on education in most states.

▼ *An engraving from 1870 of Mount Holyoke Seminary in South Hadley, Massachusetts, the first American college for women.*

*This engraving of George Peabody (seated in the center) and the board of trustees of the Peabody Education Fund was published in* Harper's Weekly *in 1867.*

## THE PEABODY EDUCATION FUND

Concerned over reports of a lack of adequate school facilities in the South, George Peabody, an American philanthropist, created the Peabody Education Fund in 1867. The fund was initially worth 3.1 million dollars, but Peabody and others made additional contributions. The fund's money went to existing school systems for construction of better facilities and the purchase of educational materials. However, because the money was given only to systems that were in existence prior to the Civil War, the fund did little to help in the education of the newly freed slaves.

## The Morrill Act

One of the most important laws affecting higher education in the United States was passed in 1862. Known as the Land Grant Act, or Morrill Act, the law granted federal land to the states to be used to create state universities, which came to be known as land grant schools. Specifically the act called for any proceeds from the land to be used for "the endowment, support, and maintenance of at least one college where the leading object shall be, without excluding other scientific and classical studies, and including military tactics, to teach such branches of learning as are related to agriculture and mechanic arts, in such manner as the legislatures of the State may respectively prescribe, in order to promote the liberal and practical education of the industrial classes in the several pursuits and professions in life." A second land grant act was passed in 1890, and eventually some 106 land grant colleges were created, including such well-known institutions as Texas A&M University, the University of Florida, and Cornell University.

*Tom Lansford*

SEE ALSO
- Amendments, Post–Civil War
- Civil Rights Acts
- Frontier Life and Culture
- Mann, Horace
- Mid-Atlantic and Chesapeake Colonies
- New England Colonies
- Northwest Ordinances • Slavery
- Southern Colonies

# Edwards, Jonathan

MANY AUTHORITIES consider Jonathan Edwards (1703–1758) the most important Protestant Christian theologian America has produced. Directly confronting the leading thinkers, philosophies, and ideas of his day, Edwards presented a case that historical Christianity was both intellectually defensible and highly relevant to the problems then facing society and the individual.

While Jonathan Edwards is regarded as a pivotal figure in—indeed the theological intellect behind—the two American religious revivals known as the Great Awakenings, his influence extends far beyond these two events. In the early eighteenth century the influence of traditional Christianity, particularly Puritanism and other forms of Calvinistic Protestantism, seemed to be fading among the English-speaking peoples of

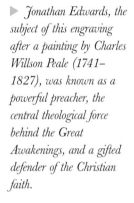

▶ *Jonathan Edwards, the subject of this engraving after a painting by Charles Willson Peale (1741–1827), was known as a powerful preacher, the central theological force behind the Great Awakenings, and a gifted defender of the Christian faith.*

the New and Old Worlds alike. Intellectuals increasingly regarded Christian faith as incapable of holding its own against the Enlightenment philosophy of John Locke or the scientific theories of Isaac Newton. Christianity was coming more and more to be considered an irrelevancy as a way of life and certainly as a way of thinking–at least by those who regarded themselves as men and women of reason.

Edwards is commonly credited with halting this trend in America, at least in his own time. He has come to be looked upon not only as a major Reformed Christian thinker and apologist but also as a man whose life and work kept historical Protestantism from being consigned to the periphery of the eighteenth-century American intellectual landscape.

## The Life of Jonathan Edwards

Jonathan Edwards grew up in East Windsor, Connecticut, the fifth of ten children born to Timothy and Esther Edwards. His father and grandfather were both ministers in New England. After receiving a bachelor's and a master's degree from Yale, in 1727 Edwards became assistant pastor to his grandfather at the church in Northampton, Massachusetts. He became its sole pastor in 1729, after his grandfather's death, and held the position until 1750. During this period Edwards's congregation experienced a "great awakening" as a result of Edwards's preaching–a particularly famous sermon being "Sinners in the Hands of an Angry God"–and of revival meetings conducted by the European evangelist George Whitefield.

*Jonathan Edwards's best-known sermon, "Sinners in the Hands of an Angry God," first preached in Ensfield, Massachusetts, on July 8, 1741, is filled with vivid imagery of the dangerous eternal situation in which sinners find themselves in relationship to a holy and just God. Many revivals and conversions were attributed to the sermon, which was soon printed and widely distributed. Although Edwards's aims were religious, not aesthetic, in nature, the sermon has come to be considered a classic of American literature.*

*There are black clouds of God's wrath now hanging directly over your heads, full of the dreadful storm, and big with thunder; and were it not for the restraining hand of God, it would immediately burst forth upon you. . . . All wicked men's pains and contrivance which they use to escape hell, while they continue to reject Christ, and so remain wicked men, do not secure them from hell one moment. Almost every natural man that hears of hell, flatters himself that he should escape it; he depends upon himself for his own security; he flatters himself in what he has done, what he is now doing, or what he intends to do. . . . And you, children, who are unconverted, do not you know that you are going down to hell, to bear the dreadful wrath of that God who is now angry with you every day and every night? . . . And let everyone that is yet out of Christ, and hanging over the pit of hell . . . now hearken to the loud calls of God's word and providence.*

Following a dispute within the congregation over the whether the Lord's Supper (the principal Protestant service of divine worship) should be open to nonbelievers—Edwards said no but lost the debate—in 1750 he and his wife, Sarah, moved to Stockbridge, Massachusetts, where he served as minister for seven years to the Mohican and Mohawk Indians. During this time some of his most significant works were written. In 1757 the trustees of Princeton University, recognizing the genius of Edwards, invited him to become its president. Although he accepted the position, he was far from being in the best of health. Since an outbreak of smallpox was raging in the Princeton environs, he was vaccinated against the disease; the vaccination weakened him so severely that he died in March 1758 at the age of fifty-four.

## The Thought of Jonathan Edwards

Edwards wrote for the philosophical community. At Yale and elsewhere, he was exposed to thinkers who were products of the Enlightenment. While never dismissing the importance and necessity of informed reason, he nevertheless considered the ideas of deism and empiricism to be unnecessary conclusions and wrote essays attempting to demonstrate that what God has revealed of himself in the Bible is actually a necessary condition for human knowledge and reason.

Edwards also wrote for the wider Christian community. His theology, expressed vividly in his writing, was rooted in classical Christianity and clearly fell within the Calvinist or wider Reformed Protestant tradition. He read and embraced the theology of the Protestant Reformers Martin Luther and John Calvin, as well as

*A sixteenth-century engraving depicting John Calvin (1509–1564), the religious reformer who was the primary theological influence on Jonathan Edwards.*

that of John Owen and other Puritans. As a Calvinist, Edwards asserted that all events, including the ultimate salvation of particular men, are meticulously ordained by a sovereign and holy God. However, Edwards was also quite committed to evangelism and the work of missions, despite the apparent tension between these activities and a belief in predestination, as he desired to see people from every tribe,

### PASSING THE WORD ALONG

The influence of Jonathan and Sarah Edwards persisted for several generations thanks to their children (eight daughters and three sons). Indeed, few families in American history have had so much influence. His daughters' husbands included lawyers and a minister-turned–college president (Aaron Burr Sr.). One of his sons became a lawyer, another a minister (he, too, became a college president), and another a politician. Edwards had seventy-two grandchildren. As his biographer Stephen Nichols put it, "His descendants are so numerous and played such significant roles that their removal might possibly have changed the course of American history."

◀ *In the foreground of this photograph is Jonathan Edwards College (founded 1932), Yale University's oldest residential college. Named for Yale's alumnus, a child prodigy who matriculated in 1716 aged only thirteen and graduated as a valedictorian four years later, the college has as its mascot a spider. This choice derives from a passage in "Sinners in the Hands of an Angry God" that describes "the God that holds you over the pit of hell, much as one holds a spider."*

tongue, and nation come to faith in Jesus Christ through the preaching of the Gospel. Some of his most significant work presented defenses of evangelistic zeal, descriptions of dramatic conversions, and even accounts of bizarre experiences from Great Awakening revivals throughout the colonies (see, for example, "Treatise concerning Religious Affections"). Edwards's more theologically challenging work, however, focused on the Calvinist-Arminian controversy, whose topic was free will. Edwards, taking the Calvinist view, argued that a man's will is bound to and determined by his corrupted nature and is not therefore able to desire God or embrace Jesus Christ as Lord and Savior apart from

the irresistible regenerating work of the Holy Spirit. Yet, he goes on to say, each man is morally responsible for his actions since he freely chooses to do what—and only what—his nature compels him to do. These ideas are developed in the treatises entitled "Freedom of the Will," "Concerning the End for Which God Created the World," and "Original Sin" and in the essay "Absolutely Sovereign: God Glorified in the Work of Redemption."

*Troy Gibson*

**SEE ALSO**
• Great Awakenings • Puritans
• Religion and Religious Movements

# Elections

AN INDIVIDUAL SERVING in elective public office—in any capacity, whether as mayor or governor, as a city council member or a congressional representative on Capitol Hill—must be elected by the voters of the political unit in which he or she is running. The means by which citizens get to make those electoral choices are interwoven with the other events in American history.

Throughout American history elections have served to determine which individuals get to serve in office at the local, state, and national levels. Chosen by the electorate at each of those levels, political officials ranging from mayors to presidents are then responsible for governing the citizens at whose behest they serve. Elections took different forms and had different consequences during the four periods of American history from its beginnings to 1877: the colonial era, the period of constitutional negotiation and ratification, the pre–Civil War period, and the Civil War and Reconstruction years.

## Elections during the Colonial Era

A central cause of the American War of Independence, which unfolded between 1776 and 1783, was the colonists' dissatisfaction with Britain's determination to tax its North American subjects without allowing them sufficient political representation. As the colonists' willingness to go to war over that point of contention would suggest, electoral progress and the political rights such progress entails were lacking in North America prior to Britain's defeat in the war and the subsequent establishment of the United States. Elections were not, however, nonexistent.

Essentially, the British struck a sensible balance between autocracy and democracy while presiding over the colonies. The monarch in London—or more accurately, his parliamentary government—had the final say over the political administration of North America, which he exercised through the governors he appointed in many but not all of the colonies. On the other hand, the British government did allow the establishment of elective representative bodies at the local level. The principle of democratic governance was first

◀ *The first elected legislative assembly in the New World was established in Jamestown, Virginia, in 1619. In 1699 its lower house, the House of Burgesses, moved to Williamsburg, where it occupied the Capitol (pictured here), the first building of its kind in America.*

established in the colonies with the formation in 1619 of a legislative body called the House of Burgesses in Jamestown, Virginia; the house was made up of two representatives from each settlement. The colonists took the first step toward formal electoral politics by selecting Captain John Smith as their leader when no one else proved capable of providing the necessary guidance to help them survive the challenging winters of 1608/1609 and 1609/1610. While Smith's selection was viewed as a solution to a temporary problem, between 1622 and 1656 William Bradford was elected to thirty-one one-year terms as governor of the Massachusetts Bay Colony in Plymouth. His tenure represented a dynasty of sorts in Plymouth.

## A GOVERNOR'S PROBLEMS

As a rule, a colonial governor was appointed to the position by the British monarch. Governors often clashed with the elected legislatures in the colonies, whose members typically called for more autonomy than the crown or its representatives in London were willing to allow. William Berkeley was one such governor. Appointed to his position by King Charles I in 1641, Berkeley (1606–1677) served one term, from 1642 to 1643, before returning to Britain to fight in a civil war, in which the king was deposed. Berkeley subsequently returned to Virginia, where he was reappointed governor by Charles II in 1660. Berkeley's loyalty to the monarchy and his unwillingness to compromise led to clashes with the House of Burgesses that eventually resulted in his recall to Britain after a rebellion led by a colonist named Nathaniel Bacon in 1676.

▲ In what became known as Bacon's Rebellion, the plantation owner Nathaniel Bacon led an uprising of colonists against William Berkeley, Virginia's unelected governor. Grievances ranged from Indian relations to economic woes. This undated engraving depicts Bacon (himself elected to the colonial legislature in 1676) confronting Berkeley.

*A contemporary illustration of Benjamin Franklin speaking at the Constitutional Convention in 1787. Sections 2, 3, and 4 of Article I of the U.S. Constitution spell out how members of the Senate and House of Representatives are to be elected; Article II, section 1, does the same for the president and vice president.*

## The Constitutional Election System

Following the American Revolution, the victors set about the task of drafting a constitution and establishing a national government for the political entity that would become the United States. Developing an electoral process proved to be a particularly divisive issue among those representing the thirteen colonies, now thirteen independent states, at the 1787 Constitutional Convention. Differences grew primarily out of the advantages, if any, that states with larger populations would have over smaller states and, similarly, how slaves residing predominantly in the South were to be counted in determin-

ing the number of representatives a state could send to the national legislative body that would become known as the Congress.

Predictably, those states with the largest populations pressed both for more representatives in the Congress and for more influence in determining who would serve as the American president. Nor was it a surprise that the southern states initially demanded that even though slaves could not vote, they still be counted as residents for purposes of representation in Congress. The delegates to the convention quickly reached a stalemate over these two issues.

Ultimately, largely through the efforts of the Virginian James Madison and Roger

Sherman of Connecticut, the delegates reached a number of interrelated compromises. The first, often called the Great Compromise, provided for a Congress composed of two bodies: a House of Representatives, whose membership was to be determined on the basis of each state's population (an advantage for the more populous states); and a Senate, made up of two representatives from each state (thus, large and small states would have equal representation). The second compromise ordained that a slave would be counted as three-fifths of a person for census and electoral purposes.

A third compromise related to the election of the nation's chief executive officer. It specified that the president would not be chosen by a direct popular vote. Rather, each state would appoint a committee of electors (their number being equal to the state's total representation in Congress). The members of this electoral college would, in light of the popular vote in their state, cast that state's votes for one candidate or another, with ties to be settled in the House.

## The Electoral College

As is the case with the system of distribution of seats in the House of Representatives, the electoral college system is a proportional one, the number of electoral votes a state casts being determined by its population. In theory (and most often in practice as well) the candidate who earns the most popular votes in the national election in a given state also earns all of that state's electoral votes. Technically, though, electors can cast their votes for whomever they wish when the college convenes for a formal count following

the popular election. In addition, should the electoral vote end in a tie, the president is chosen by a vote of the members of the House of Representatives.

▲ *An unattributed portrait of James Madison, who played a central role at the Constitutional Convention and contributed to the Great Compromise.*

### THE SECRET BALLOT

Voting by secret ballot is now the rule in virtually every election, in the United States and elsewhere, but the practice is of relatively recent origin and was surrounded by controversy when it was proposed.

The use of the secret ballot was first proposed in 1838 by a group of British political reformers known as Chartists. The first use of secret balloting appears to have taken place in the British colony of Tasmania (now one of the states that constitute Australia) in February 1856. By April of that year, the secret ballot was put into effect throughout Australia.

Although the secret-ballot idea quickly crossed the Atlantic, it took a long time to root itself in American political soil: the first president of the United States elected by Australian ballot, as the secret ballot came to be known, was Grover Cleveland in 1892.

### The Elections of 1796 and 1800

In the first two U.S. elections George Washington, the commander of the Continental army during the American Revolution, ran unopposed. Following Washington's decision not to seek a third term in 1796, Thomas Jefferson of Virginia and John Adams of Massachusetts were

*▶ John Quincy Adams, pictured here in a painting by George Peter Alexander Healy (1813–1894), won the election of 1824 under suspicious circumstances. After the voting in the electoral college failed to yield a majority of votes for any candidate, the election was thrown into the House of Representatives. Opponents cried foul when Henry Clay, having endorsed Adams in the House, was rewarded with the prized office of secretary of state—which had so often been a stepping-stone to the presidency.*

opponents in the nation's first contested presidential race. The race featured parties with two distinctive political philosophies. Adams's Federalists favored a strong federal government that would have a say in all affairs of state, particularly those pertaining to economics; Federalists were strongest in the New England states. Democratic-Republicans were advocates of states' rights, an issue that was of particular concern to voters in the West and the South.

Adams won the 1796 race by three electoral votes; when he ran for reelection in 1800, he lost to Jefferson. In the latter race, Jefferson and his running mate, Aaron Burr, were listed on the same ballot and thus received the same number of electoral votes. The deadlock was broken in Jefferson's favor, albeit only after thirty-six ballots in the House.

### Other Elections during the Pre–Civil War Years

The opposition of a Federalist and a Democratic-Republican was the norm in subsequent elections through 1812. With the disappearance of the Federalist Party as a political force, later races tended to focus less on parties and more on issues, especially the deepening divide between the

### POLITICAL CONVENTIONS

Political conventions serve as the formal means through which parties nominate their candidate for president every four years. Nowadays, conventions act largely as a rubber stamp applied to the already victorious candidate. In nineteenth-century America, however, conventions were virtually always consequential affairs. The delegates attending a convention, whatever the party, often engaged in substantive debates before deciding on the party's nominee. The process might take several ballots. In addition, the choice of a vice presidential candidate, although typically an afterthought, proved quite significant on several occasions. In the first century of the American republic's existence, three vice presidents succeeded to the presidency when the incumbent died in office: John Tyler replaced William Henry Harrison in 1841, Millard Fillmore replaced Zachary Taylor in 1850, and Andrew Johnson replaced Lincoln in 1865.

North and the South over slavery. Two notable political developments in subsequent years were the transformation of the Democratic-Republican Party into the Democratic Party under Andrew Jackson, the populist hero of the War of 1812, and the establishment of the Republican Party, with its staunch antislavery platform adopted from the Whigs, in 1854. Jackson served two successive terms in office, from 1829 to 1837. The first Republican president was Abraham Lincoln, elected in 1860. Within months of that election, eleven southern states had seceded from the Union, and the United States was embroiled in the Civil War.

▼ *This 1867 woodcut depicts freedmen, having been brought to the polls by so-called carpetbaggers, voting in New Orleans.*

## Elections during the Civil War and Reconstruction Years

The electoral environment in the United States during the Civil War was deeply affected by the secession of the southern states from the Union. Replacing the North-South divisions in electoral politics, a significant rift opened between Lincoln's Republicans and the northern Democrats, albeit one that did not prevent Lincoln's reelection in the fall of 1864, as the tide of war shifted decisively in favor of the Union. Lincoln's assassination within a week of the South's surrender in April 1865 ushered in not only a new president, Andrew Johnson, but also (and more significantly) the Reconstruction era, which embodied revolutionary electoral changes.

*In the aftermath of the Civil War, Congress passed three constitutional amendments, the Thirteenth, Fourteenth, and Fifteenth, to secure the rights of former slaves, particularly those who continued to reside in the South. The right to vote–a right often violated in practice–was guaranteed to them with the ratification of the Fifteenth Amendment in 1870.*

*The right of citizens of the United States to vote shall not be denied or abridged by the United States or by any State on account of race, color, or previous condition of servitude.*

FIFTEENTH AMENDMENT, ARTICLE 1

The most significant alteration to electoral policy during Reconstruction was the ratification of the Fifteenth Amendment in 1870. The amendment granted former slaves the right to vote by prohibiting the use of race as a determinant of one's eligibility to vote. In response to continuing southern discrimination against black voters, the Republican-controlled Congress passed the Enforcement Acts in 1870 and 1871. These acts placed all congressional elections under federal governmental control and authorized the use of the military to enforce voting rights for blacks.

▼ *Senator Thomas Ferry announces the results of the 1876 election between Rutherford B. Hayes and Samuel J. Tilden. The final vote, which declared Hayes the new president by one electoral vote, could not be announced until four o'clock in the morning on March 2, 1877.*

**The End of Reconstruction**

The Reconstruction era closed in 1876 with a major electoral controversy. In that year's presidential election Samuel Tilden, the Democratic candidate, clearly defeated the Republican Rutherford B. Hayes in the popular vote, but Hayes gained the White House by means of a deal in the electoral college. In return for being awarded all the votes in dispute, Hayes promised to withdraw all federal troops from the South once he took office. That deal not only ended Reconstruction but opened the door to decades of lax enforcement of the voting rights guaranteed by the Fifteenth Amendment.

*Robert J. Pauly Jr.*

**SEE ALSO**

- Amendments, Post–Civil War
- Burr, Aaron
- Constitution of the United States
- Continental Congresses
- Democratic Party • Jackson, Andrew
- Jefferson, Thomas • Reconstruction
- Republican Party • State Constitutions
- States' Rights
- Third Parties and Alternative Political Movements • Washington, George
- Whig Party • Women's Rights

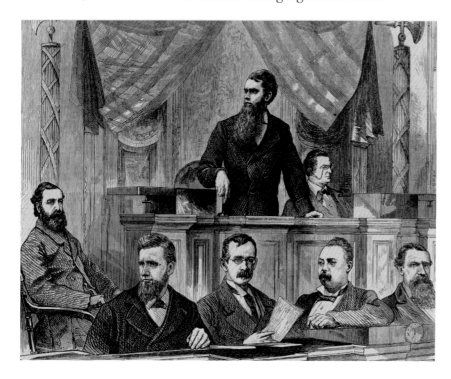

# Guided Research

*These Internet and print resources will support a wide range of research needs in American history.*

## Internet

American Memory Historical Collections, Library of Congress. **http://memory.loc.gov/ammem/index.html.** Documents, exhibits, maps, photographs, prints, recordings, and motion pictures.

Best of History Web Sites. **www.besthistorysites.net.** Annotated links to history Web sites; history lesson plans (K–12), teacher guides, and activities.

The Learning Page, Library of Congress. **http://memory.loc.gov/learn.** Activities, tools, ideas, and features for students and educators.

Liberty Library of Constitutional Classics. **www.constitution.org/liberlib.htm.** Primary materials related to the Constitution, earlier documents that influenced it, and books on constitutional interpretation.

## Print

*The American Republic: Primary Sources.* Edited by Bruce Frohnen. Indianapolis, 2002. Documents and archival writings on U.S. history.

*Founding the Republic: A Documentary History.* Edited by John J. Patrick. Westport, CT, 1995. Famous and forgotten views on the Revolution and the creation of the U.S political system.

*Opposing Viewpoints in American History: From Colonial Times to Reconstruction.* Edited by William Dudley. Farmington Hills, MI, 2006. Essays by contemporary figures with differing perspectives on critical events.

*Retracing the Past: Readings in the History of the American People.* Vol. 1, *To 1877.* 6th ed. Edited by Gary B. Nash and Ronald B. Schultz. New York, 2006. Sources that highlight social history and the experiences of minorities and women.

---

*These resources will aid those wishing to learn more about topics covered in this volume.*

COMMUNICATION
Crowley, David, and Paul Heyer. *Communication in History: Technology, Culture, Society.* 4th ed. Boston, 2003.

COMPROMISE OF 1850
Hamilton, Holman. *Prologue to Conflict: The Crisis and Compromise of 1850.* Lexington, KY, 1964.

CONFEDERATE STATES OF AMERICA
Davis, William. *Look Away: A History of the Confederate States of America.* New York, 2003.

Ranson, Roger. *The Confederate States of America: What Might Have Been.* New York, 2005.

CONSTITUTION OF THE UNITED STATES
Madison, James. *Notes of the Debates in the Federal Convention of 1787.* Edited by Adrienne Koch. New York, 1987.

McDonald, Forrest. *Novus Ordo Seclorum: The Intellectual Origins of the Constitution.* Lawrence, KS, 1985.

CONTINENTAL CONGRESSES
Henderson, James. *Party Politics in the Continental Congress.* New York, 1974.

Montross, Lynn. *The Reluctant Rebels: The Story of the Continental Congress, 1774–1789.* New York, 1950.

COOPER, JAMES FENIMORE
Darnell, Donald. *James Fenimore Cooper: Novelist of Manners.* Newark, NJ, 1993.

CROCKETT, DAVID
Derr, Mark. *The Frontiersman: The Real Life and the Many Legends of Davy Crockett.* New York, 1993.

CUFFE, PAUL
Thomas, Lamont D. *Rise to Be a People: A Biography of Paul Cuffe.* Urbana, IL, 1986.

CUSTER, GEORGE ARMSTRONG
Wert, Jeffry D. *Custer: The Controversial Life of George Armstrong Custer.* New York, 1996.

DAVIS, JEFFERSON
Cooper, William J., Jr. *Jefferson Davis, American.* New York, 2001.

DECLARATION OF INDEPENDENCE
Latham, Earl, ed. *The Declaration of Independence and the Constitution.* Lexington, MA, 1976.

Malone, Dumas. *The Story of the Declaration of Independence.* New York, 1975.

DEMOCRACY IN AMERICA
Manent, Pierre. *Tocqueville and the Nature of Democracy.* Lanham, MD, 1996.

DEMOCRATIC PARTY
Remini, Robert V. *Martin Van Buren and the Making of the Democratic Party.* New York, 1970.

DIX, DOROTHEA
Brown, Thomas. *Dorothea Dix: New England Reformer.* Cambridge, MA, 1998.

DOUGLAS, STEPHEN A.
Meyer, Daniel. *Stephen A. Douglas and the American Union.* Chicago, 1994.

DOUGLASS, FREDERICK
McFeely, William S. *Frederick Douglass.* New York, 1991.

DRED SCOTT V. SANDFORD
Rehnquist, William H. *The Supreme Court: How It Was, How It Is.* New York, 1987.

DUTCH COLONIZATION
Shorto, Russell. *The Island at the Center of the World: The Epic Story of Dutch Manhattan and the Forgotten Colony That Shaped America.* New York, 2004.

EDUCATION
Anderson, James D. *The Education of Blacks in the South, 1860–1935.* Chapel Hill, NC, 1988.

Ryan, Patrick. *Historical Foundations of Public Education in America.* Dubuque, IA, 1965.

EDWARDS, JONATHAN
Marsden, George. *Jonathan Edwards: A Life.* New Haven, CT, 2003.

ELECTIONS
Crittenden, John A. *Parties and Elections in the United States.* New York, 1988.

# Glossary

**amnesty** An official pardon granted to a large group of people who have, or may have, committed an offense (usually of a political rather than criminal nature).

**aristocracy** Government by a landed or otherwise privileged class, often hereditary in nature. The term is sometimes used loosely to refer the most powerful members of a society.

**bicameral** A term used to describe a legislative body having two branches, chambers, or houses.

**circuit court** A kind of American state or federal court that sits in more than one place in a given judicial district.

**deism** An Enlightenment-influenced form of religion that acknowledged the existence of a divine creator but denied his continuing involvement in the universe he had shaped.

**despotism** A government or political system in which the ruler exercises absolute power.

**elector** A member of an electoral college. In the United States, the electors of each state, on the basis of the popular vote in the general election, cast their votes (normally on a winner-take-all basis) to choose the president.

**empiricism** In religion and philosophy, a form of skepticism, originating in the seventeenth century, which in its radical form holds that all knowledge derives from the senses and that nothing is knowable that does not proceed from experience.

**Enlightenment** An important intellectual movement of eighteenth-century Europe that rejected traditional social, political, and religious arrangements and ideas in favor of new ones that were claimed to be based in logic, reason, and scientific observation.

**excise** A tax on the manufacture, sale, or use of goods or on the carrying on of an occupation or activity.

**freeman** In much of the antebellum United States, a term with the special meaning "a free black man or woman." Such a freeman did not generally have the rights of citizenship.

**impost** A customs duty or tax.

**libel** The publication of false information with the intent of damaging a person's reputation or position.

**malaria** A parasitic disease that attacks red blood cells and causes a recurring fever. Malaria is transmitted by mosquitos and is therefore often associated with marshes and other areas where standing water is found.

**manumit** To free someone from slavery.

**matériel** Military supplies or equipment, especially guns and ammunition.

**nullification** In American history, the action of an individual state or states to nullify, or declare null and void, a law enacted by the federal government.

**patroon** In the areas of Dutch settlement in the New World, the proprietor of a landed estate whose rights were often similar to those of a feudal lord.

**plantation** A significant plot of land, often in the thousands of acres, on which cash crops, such as cotton and tobacco, are cultivated by workers who live on the land. Most plantations in the United States were in the South, and many relied on slave labor.

**plurality** In an election of more than two candidates, the number of votes obtained by the top vote getter, if he or she does not receive an absolute majority of 50 percent plus one.

**populist** A politician who seeks to draw support primarily from the common people and claims to stand for their interests.

**proprietor** In American colonial history, a person who received from the British crown the grant of full ownership of a colony, whereby he had the right to form a government and distribute land as he saw fit.

**sawyer** Someone who processes trees into usable lumber.

**social-contract theory** An eighteenth-century theory of governance that assumes that individuals agree to be governed and, in return, the government agrees to protect their rights.

**sovereignty** Autonomy; freedom from external control.

**typhoid fever** An infection caused by a bacteria and characterized by intestinal distress, rashes, and a high fever. Before the development of antibiotics, typhoid fever was often fatal.

**unalienable** In a legal context, not surrenderable or transferable; thus, unalienable rights are rights that can neither be taken nor be given away.

**wampum** Beads of polished shells strung in strands, belts, or sashes and used by North American Indians as money, ceremonial pledges, and ornaments.

# Index

Page numbers in **boldface** type refer to entire articles. Page numbers in *italic* type refer to illustrations.

**A**bolitionism 300, 302–304, 305, 308, 331
Adams, John *257,* 279, 288, 330
Adams, John Quincy 287, *288,* 289, 291, *330*
Adams, Samuel 254, *257*
African Americans 291, 305, 306, 308, 332
　Cuffe 266–268
　Douglass 300–304
　*see also* slavery
Alamo, Battle of the 263, 264–265
Alien and Sedition Acts 288
Anglo-Dutch Wars 312, 314
Anti-Federalists 250
Articles of Confederation 230, 238, 240
　Constitution 246, 247, 249, 250, 251, 253
　Continental Congresses 256–257, 258

**B**acon's Rebellion 327
ballot, secret (Australian) 329
Bell, Alexander Graham 232, *233*
Benjamin, Judah P. 244, *245*
bicameralism 247, 249, 329
Boston Tea Party 277–278
Bradford, William 327
Breckenridge, John C. 298, *299*
British colonization 255, 256, 312, 313, 314
　communication 228–230
　Declaration of Independence 277–283
　education 315–316
　elections 326–327, 329
Brown, John 237, 300, 304

**C**alhoun, John C. 237, 241, 289, 290, 291
Calvinism 322, 324, 325

checks and balances 252
Civil Rights Acts 291, 320
Civil War 290, 305, 307, 308, 331
　turning points 241
　women nurses 294–295
　*see also* Confederate States of America
Clay, Henry 241, 298, *330*
　Missouri Compromise 234
Coercive Acts 253, 255, 277
colonial wars 261, 312, 314
　*see also* Indian Wars
*Common Sense* (Paine) 278, 279, 282
communication **228–233**
Compromise of 1850 **234–236,** 274, 298
Confederate States of America **237–245,** 272, 274, 276, 290, 308
Congress 231, 234, 237, 332
　Constitution 247, 248–250, 251, 252, 290
　elections 328–329
　*see also* Continental Congresses; legislative system
Constitution of the United States **246–252,** 253, 280, 282, 283, *285,* 287, 302, 305, 306–307, 328, 329
　interpretation 290, 300, 302
　states' rights 237, 245, 249, 288, 290
Continental Congresses **253–259,** 279, 280, 318
　limited powers 246
　post office 230, 232
　*see also* Congress
Cooper, James Fenimore **260–262**
Cooper, Susan 260, 261
cotton 239–240, 242
Crockett, David **263–265**
Cuffe, Paul **266–268**
Curtis, Benjamin 306, 307
Custer, George Armstrong **269–271**

**D**avis, Jefferson 239, 240, 241, 242, 243, 244–245, **272–276**

Declaration of Independence 237, 256, **277–283,** 308
　signers 254, *257,* 280
*Democracy in America* (Tocqueville) **284–286**
Democratic Party **287–291,** 296, 298–299, 331
Democratic-Republicans 287–288, 289, 291, 330–331
Dix, Dorothea **292–295**
Douglas, Stephen A. 236, **296–299**
Douglass, Frederick 235, **300–304**
*Dred Scott v. Sandford* **305–308**
Dutch colonization **309–314**

**E**ducation **315–321**
Edwards, Jonathan **322–325**
elections 249, **326–332**
　party system 288, 291
　*see also* representation
electoral college 249, 289, 329, *330,* 332
Emancipation Proclamation 303
Enlightenment 280–283, 323, 324
evangelism 323, 324–325
executive system 249, 251, 252, 253, 282, 329
expansion and Manifest Destiny 297–298, 305, 306
　Compromise of 1850 234–236

**F**ederalism 251
*Federalist Papers* 250, *251*
Federalists 250, 287, 288, 289, 291, 330
Fifteenth Amendment 291, 320, 332
flags, Confederate 241
Fourteenth Amendment 276, 291, 303, 320, 332
France 256, 259, 262, 284–286, 287
　Quasi War 288, 289
Franklin, Benjamin 230, 232, 256, 279, 317, *328*
French and Indian War 261

frontier life and culture 230–231, 246, 321
　Cooper portrayals 260–262
　Crockett 263–265
Fugitive Slave Laws 234
fur trade 309, 310, 312

**G**reat Awakenings 322, 323, 325
Great Britain, relations with 243, 249, 305, 307
Greeley, Horace 230, 276

**H**amilton, Alexander 250, *251,* 287, 290
Hamilton, Andrew 229
Hancock, John 254, 256, *257,* 280
Harpers Ferry raid 300, 304
Harvard University 315, 316, 317, 319
Hayes, Rutherford B. *290,* 291, 332
House of Burgesses 279, *326,* 327
Hudson, Henry 309, *310,* 312

**I**mpeachment 252, 307
Indian wars 263, 269, 270–271, 272–273, 312

**J**ackson, Andrew 241, 263, 264, 287, *288,* 289–290, 291, 296, 297, 331
Jackson, Thomas J. ("Stonewall") 245
Jamestown 309, 315, *326,* 327
Jay, John 250, *251*
Jefferson, Thomas 241, 256, 272, 287, 290, 305, 330
　Declaration of Independence 256, 279–280, 281, 282, 308
　education theory 318
　states' rights 289, 291
Johnson, Andrew 276, 290, 291, 307, 330, 331
judicial system 249, 250, 251, 252, 320
　slave status 305, 306–308
jury trial 282

Kansas-Nebraska Act 298, 346
kindergartens 319

Land-grant schools 318, 319, 321
Lee, Richard Henry *257*, 279, 281
Lee, Robert E. 145, 244, 245, 269, 274, 308
legislative system 256–257, 285, *326, 327 see also* Congress
Lincoln, Abraham 230, 232, 237, 241, 242, 244, 274, 290, 291, 299, 303, 331
  Douglas debates 296, 297, 298
literature 260–262, 323
Little Bighorn 269, 270–271

Madison, James 247, 248, *249*, 250, *251*, 289, 298, 328, *329*
mail 228–231, 232, 233
Manhattan Island 310, 311, 312
Mann, Horace 319
mental illness 292, 293–294, 295
mercantilism and colonial economies 255, 277–278
  Dutch colonies 310, 314
Mexican War 235, 273, 291, 297–298
Minuit, Peter 311, 312
Missouri Compromise 234, 289, 291, 306–307
Mohawks 312, 324
Mohicans 261, 262, 324
Monroe, James 289, 291
Morrill Act 321
Morse, Samuel F. B. 231
Morse code 231, 232

Native Americans 228, 238, 290, 309, 310, 311, 312, 314, 324
  Cooper portrayals 261, 262
  *see also* Indian wars
natural law 281, 282
Navigation Acts 277
New Amsterdam 309, 310, 311, 314
New England colonies 312, 314, 323–325, 327

African Americans 266–267
Coercive Acts 255, 277–278
communications 228, 229
education 315–316, 317, 319
New Jersey Plan 249
New Netherland 309–314
Northwest Ordinance 305, 318
nullification 290
nurses 294–295

Oberlin College 319

Paine, Thomas 278, 279, 282
Paterson, William 258, 259
Peach War 312
Pius IX, Pope 275
Pony Express 230, 231, 232
popular sovereignty 235, 236, 298
postal system 228–230, 232
presidency *see* executive system
prison reform 292, 293
Protestantism 313, 322–325
Puritans 315, 322, 324

Quakers 266, 267
Quasi War 288, 289

Railroads 230–231, 232, 233
Randolph, Edmund 248–249
Randolph, Peyton 254, 255–256
Reconstruction 291, 303, 320, 331, 332
religion and religious movements 292
  Dutch colonies 310–311, 312, 313
  education 315, 317, 318
  Edwards 322–325
  representation 254, 258, 327, 328–329
  proportional 234, 329
  slave states 249–250, 329
  taxation without 267, 282, 326
Republican Party 237, 291, 331
Revolutionary War 237, 246, 249, 266, 318, 326
  African Americans 267, 366
  Continental Congresses 253, 255, 258

*see also* Declaration of Independence
Roman Catholic Church 275

Scott, Dred 305–308
secession 237, 238, 239, 241, 244, 245, 274, 276, 290, 291, 296, 299, 308, 331
separation of powers 251, 252
Sherman, Roger 248, 279, 328–329
slavery 238, 244, 319, 320
  Constitution 247, 249–250, 302, 329
  Democratic Party 287, 289, 291
  Douglas 296, 297, 298
  Douglass 300–302
  Dred Scott case 305–308
  expansion into territories 234–236, 290, 297–298, 305
  Republican Party 237, 331
Smith, John 327
states' rights 249, 251, 253, 290, 291, 330
  Confederacy 237, 238, 242, 243, 245, 276
  Virginia and Kentucky Resolutions 288–289
Stephens, Alexander 241, 242, 243, 244, *245*
Stuyvesant, Peter 311, 312, 313, 314
suffrage 267, 291, 302, 303, 332
Supreme Court, U.S. 250, 320
  Dred Scott case 305, 306–308

Taney, Roger B. 306, *307*, 308
tariffs 238–239, 240, 247, 290, 291
taxation 240, 246, 247, 249, 250, 257, 282, 289, 316
  without representation 267, 282, 326
Taylor, Zachary 272, 273
telegraph 230, 231, 232, 233
telephone 232–233
Thirteenth Amendment 320, 332
Thomson, Charles 254

Tilden, Samuel *290*, 291, 332
Tocqueville, Alexis de 284–286
trade 240, 247, 249, 266–267
  Dutch colonies 309, 310, 312, 314

Unicameralism 253, 256–257

Van Buren, Martin 289, 291
veto 239, 249, 252, 257, 291
Virginia and Kentucky Resolutions 237, 288–289
Virginia Plan 248–249

Washington, George 241, 254, 256, 258
  Constitution 246–247, 248
  presidency 287, 330
West India Company 310, 311, 312
Whig Party 264, 331
William and Mary College 316, 317
women 240, 293–295
women's rights 302, 304, 319, 320

Yale University *318*, 319, 323, 324, *325*